6.95

HANG GLIDING TECHNIQUES

D0870670

by DENNIS PAGEN

YANKTON
COMMUNITY LIBRARY
DISCARD
JUN 18 1991
YANKTON, SO. DAK. 57078

ILLUSTRATIONS BY THE AUTHOR

First Edition Copyright © 1978 by Dennis Pagen

Revised Edition Copyright © 1982 by Dennis Pagen
All Rights Reserved

First Printing: August, 1982
Printed in the United States of America

Published by Dennis Pagen
P.O. Box 601, State College, Pa. 16801

ISBN 0-936310-05-7

85545

CONTENTS

FORWARD

The fields behind my childhood home were visited frequently by Broad-winged and Red-shouldered hawks. I sat for hours on the sunny hillside watching these lucky souls circle, soar and climb in the mysterious air currents. I longed to join them. Little did I know that my fantasies would be realized and I too would ride the wind on silent wings. For me, hang gliding is the realization of my childhood dream.

The process of learning the freedom of the skies was a gradual one. Trial and error played no small role. The problem was a lack of instructors (the hawks weren't interested in teaching a beginner). When my friends and I started flying, there were few well understood techniques and even fewer open paths of communication in the sport. We learned to do turns out of necessity – a row of trees crossed our flight path. Other flying skills were acquired in an equally haphazard, hit and miss fashion (sometimes more hit than miss). I am happy to have survived the experience.

Today a beginner has access to plenty of expert guidance. There are certified schools and excellent manuals to help him understand the conditions and learn the skills necessary for safe flight. However, a vacuum exists at the more advanced level.

Very few pilots take instruction beyond the beginning level. Indeed, few instructors are qualified to teach advanced skills. After a pilot passes the beginning stage, he is in a position very similar to that of my friends and I in the early days of hang gliding. Learning more advanced skills consists of watching others, asking questions and random practice. Not the best way to progress by any means. This book is an attempt to correct this situation.

The material in the following pages will help you familiarize yourself with your glider and become completely at home in the sky. Details of all aspects of advanced hang gliding are included. It is assumed that the reader has an understanding of simple hang gliding terminology and micrometeorology. If this is not the case, two previous books by the author, *Hang Gliding Flying Skills* and *Flying Conditions*, are recommended. It is important to master the basics before trying to progress to more advanced levels.

In truth, we are all beginners compared to our feathered mentors, the birds. We should never stop learning as long as we continue to fly. No manual can expose a pilot to everything there is to experience in the air. However, this book will be successful if it carries you one step further in the pursuit of freedom in flight.

AUTHOR'S NOTE

A portion of the material in this book appeared in the book entitled *Hang Gliding for Advanced Pilots*. However, as the practice of hang gliding progressed over the years, skills that were once considered advanced have become part of the intermediate learning process. Thus, a new title was in order. In addition, more information and new design factors have appeared since the book was originally written. Thus, a large part of the material on thermal flying as well as cross country and equipment considerations is completely new while other parts have been upgraded and revised. In all, approximately 40% of the material in this book did not appear in the original edition. I hope pilots of all levels find an idea or two herein to enhance their understanding of flight. If so, this effort will be considered a success.

Dennis Pagen

State College, Pennsylvania
August 13, 1982

CHAPTER I

STRAIGHT AND LEVEL

Hang gliding is exciting for beginner and expert alike. The weekend pilot can have as much fun as the professional flyer, for the challenges and rewards start with the first ground skimming flight. However, very early in his hang gliding career, almost every pilot wants to improve his flying abilities to the advanced stage.

To accomplish this improvement, two equally important practices must occur. First, a pilot must accumulate airtime. This means many flights in various terrains and conditions. On each flight one should learn a little more about the control of his craft and the ways of the wind. A pilot must learn to relax in the air so that he can concentrate on detecting lift and perfecting maneuvers. Turns and speed control are especially important. The ultimate goal is to reach a point where the aluminum and Dacron wings are an extension of the body. When this is achieved the pilot reacts immediately and correctly to every new situation.

The second requirement for advancing one's skills consists of study. This means learning as much as possible from books, magazines and fellow pilots (this includes the birds). There is so much to learn about guiding an aircraft through the air, that we can only acquire all the understanding necessary by reading or asking questions. Experiences of other pilots can teach us much more readily than if we went out to look for a certain flying situation. It is only through a complete understanding of the environment and our gliders that the full potentials of flight can be met.

In this chapter, we will cover the basic controls that all pilots must perfect to the highest degree. This material is very important, since every flight is a combination of decisions and these basic controls. Making wise decisions and perfect controls produces efficient flight, which in turn awards the pilot with freedom in the sky. This is the essence of hang gliding.

PITCH CONTROL

When we speak of flight control, we are referring to pitch and roll control, front-to-back and side-to-side movement of the control bar, respectively. Pulling in or pushing out on the control bar results in pitch or angle of attack changes. Moving the bar to one side changes the glider's angle of bank. Almost every maneuver possible on a hang glider is performed by some combination of pitch and roll.

A third motion a glider can undergo is termed "yawing." This is a rotation about a vertical axis. In general, yaw control is automatically taken care of by the glider design. The pilot cannot yaw the glider to any great extent. However, advanced turns can be performed using a yawing technique. This is discussed in a later section. Figure 1 shows the three types of motion possible on a glider.

The first thing a hang glider pilot learns is pitch control – adjusting for speed and flaring for landing. For more advanced flight, much more is required. The glider's pitching characteristics must be understood in three separate situations: turbulence, turns and speed control. The first two will be discussed at length in later sections.

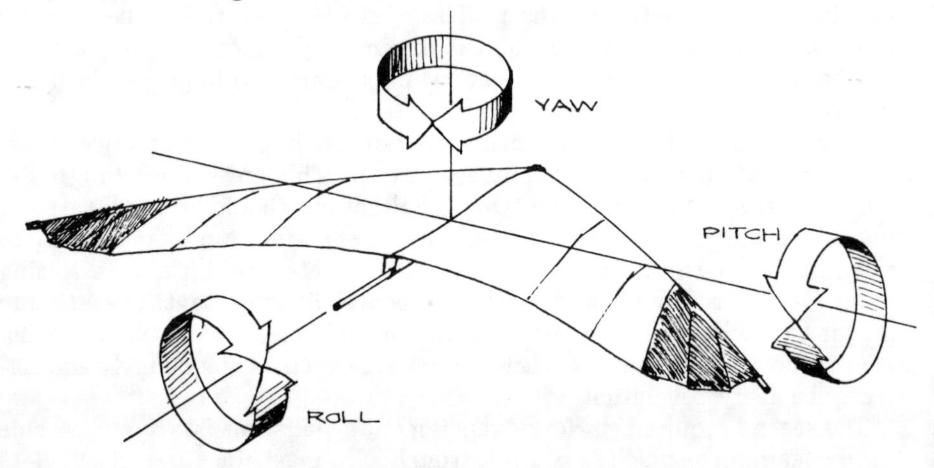

Figure 1 · Axis of Motion

Speed control in straight ahead flight is important in order to maximize flight distance and take advantage of lifting conditions. There are four cardinal speeds on a glider. These are: stall speed, minimum sink speed, best glide speed and maximum safe flying speed. Note that flying speed in a glider is directly related to angle of attack or control bar position (the higher the angle of attack, the slower the flight speed, and vice versa). Consequently, we will often speak of the angle of attack or control bar position for stalling, minimum sink, etc. Now we will find out how to determine and use our glider's four cardinal speeds.

MAXIMUM SAFE FLYING SPEED

The "maximum safe flying speed" is not critical in smooth air. Although airplanes can enter dives that can tear the wings off due to the excessive loads when pulling up, it is our happy fate that most hang gliders are incapable of such a feat. The load is limited by the fact that a stall occurs in the wing, which greatly reduces lift and conseqeuntly, loading.

The equation: $\left(\frac{\text{flying speed}}{\text{stall speed}}\right)^2$ = maximum load factor gives the ultimate load in Gs that an aircraft can experience with a given flying speed. One G equals the total weight of the pilot and glider combined. Assuming that a certain hang glider stalls at 18 mph, then one can fly at 44 mph and create a 6G load $(\frac{44}{18})^2 = 6$ with a sudden push out on the control bar. Similarly, and 8G load could be achieved if flying speed was 51 mph.

In actual practice, however, a modern glider does not experience as much loading as indicated by the mathematical analysis, for the flexible leading edges bow in and relieve a large part of the additional load. In most cases, a pilot can "bury the bar" to his knees (if prone) or chest (if seated), then push out rapidly without fear of reaching a glider's structural limits. Moving beyond the limits of normal arm extension – that is, by crawling forward on the front cables – is a risky practice at best for there is a danger of falling in front of the control bar and the excess speed increases the effects of turbulence. There should be no flying situation (competition or otherwise) that requires such falcon-like dives. Keep your high speed work within the limits of your reach and confined to smooth air, and you will be safe.

Of course, the foregoing guideline assumes that your glider is pitch stable (non-divergent). That is, at high speeds, with the bar pulled in, the glider should have a tendency to nose up (slow up) and pull the bar back out. A glider that does not do this may stabilize in a steep dive or even tuck under and tumble. Every hang glider sold by a reputable manufacturer should be well tested and devoid of divergent tendencies. However, for your own assurance, you can test your glider yourself. Simply start pulling in on the control bar on a flight in smooth air with lots of ground clearance.

As you pull in gradually, note the force required to hold the control bar in. The more you pull in, the greater should be the force you have to exert.

Proceed in this manner until you reach top speed. If at any point you feel the control bar pressure get lighter, ease the bar back out to slow up. Repeat the process and look for the change in pressure to occur at the same place, to be certain that the reduction in control bar force was not due to random air movement. A glider that repeatedly exhibits a reduced control bar force as you pull the bar in should be held in suspicion. It is best to put the glider on a test vehicle to determine the source of the problem. The glider may simply be out of trim – which is easily corrected – or of faulty design. In case of the latter, the addition of defined tips is sometimes a successful remedy. Defined tips are wing tips whose downward deflection is limited in some manner. Thus, at high speed (low angles of attack) the tips create less lift and more drag than the center section of the wing, which results in a strong nose-up force. Figure 2 depicts an example of defined tip mechanisms.

If your glider does not display the tendency to lighten in control bar pressure as you pull in, then you can consider it to be stable or non-divergent throughout the range of normal flight. This does not mean that your glider is pitch positive (non-divergent) for every angle of attack. In fact, most wings will tuck under given sufficient rotational velocity, whether from extreme turbulence or radical maneuvers. However, if a pilot minds his business and avoids the preceding two flying pitfalls, he should feel quite safe flying a modern design glider at normal flight speeds.

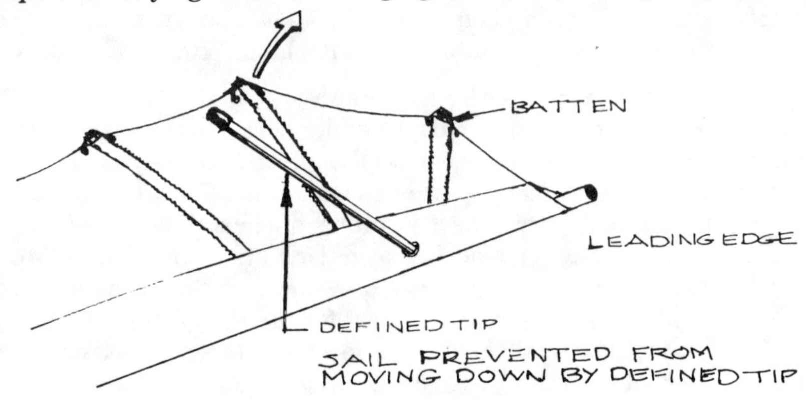

Figure 2 · Defined Tip

Flying in turbulence is another matter. Just as you slow your car down on a rutted road, or throttle back your boat in heavy chop, you should reduce flying speed in turbulence. The faster you fly, the rougher the air feels. What appears to be unsteady rising and falling at a slow speed will feel like heavy pounding at a high speed. The reason this occurs is that turbulent air moves in a random fashion so that when you fly through it, your angle of attack is constantly being changed. Recall that changing the angle of attack on a wing section also changes the lift and drag created. The constantly changing lift and drag is what gives you the bounces. The quicker these changes come (that is, the faster you fly), the greater the forces due to acceleration, somewhat like the greater force experienced in a quick, sharp turn as opposed to that of a slow gradual turn in a car.

The conclusion to draw from the above is that the "maximum safe flying speed" is a good bit less in turbulent air than in smooth air. How much less? That depends on the severity of the turbulence. In turbulence of any degree, you never know whether or not the strongest blast in the air will hit you at the next flap of your wings. Therefore it is wise to slow down as much as possible. If you slow too much, you risk turbulence induced stalls and of course, loss of control. The best speed to fly is near the "best glide speed." This will ease the bumps yet still provide good maneuverability. The "maximum safe flying speed" in turbulence then can be assumed to be a few miles per hour faster than the "best glide speed."

In truth, there is little premium in flying at high speeds. As we shall see in subsequent chapters, cross-country flying in a hang glider does not require high speeds. Furthermore, speed runs in competition should definitely not take place if the air is turbulent. Flying at top speed may be necessary when trying to penetrate a high wind, but in this case, the pilot made a judgment error by taking off in such vigorous conditions in the first place.

Although reduction of stresses on the aircraft is often given as the reason for slowing down in turbulence, there is a more important reason for hang glider pilots to fly slow. This is to maintain control. With the typical flexible suspension system and weight shift control, a hang glider pilot is not in command of his ship when turbulence slackens his harness lines or fatigues his arms by requiring constant corrections. Slowing down in turbulence minimizes the risk of sail inversions and reduces the force needed to keep the glider on an even keel. Turbulence is our number one enemy, but we can quell the ferocity of the beast by taking things nice and easy.

BEST GLIDE SPEED

Every aircraft has an airspeed at which the ratio of lift to drag is a maximum. This is written as L / D max and is equal to glider's best glide ratio. Glide ratio and L / D are used interchangeably in discussions of a glider's performance. Figure 3 shows why this is so. The drag (D) is directed (by convention) exactly opposite to the direction of flight. Also by convention, the lift force (L) is assumed to be perpendicular to the drag. The sum of these two forces (R) must equal the total weight (W) in steady flight. Since the direction and speed of the glider (V) is parallel to (D), it can be seen that he angle x is equal to angle y. Thus, from the laws of similar triangles, Vh / Vv = L / D. The horizontal velocity (Vh) and the vertical velocity (Vv) is proportional to the horizontal and vertical distance covered respectively. Therefore, we can say that the glide ratio equals Vh / Vv as well as L / D. This equality holds true except when the glider is accelerating or decelerating, that is, changing velocity. We call L / D max our best glide ratio and express it as a numerical ratio such as, 8 to 1.

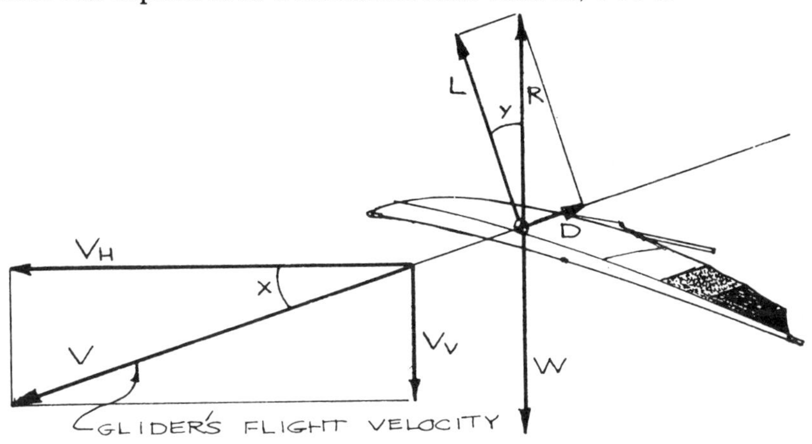

Figure 3 - Glide Ratio and L/D

In Figure 3, the relationship of the velocity and forces is shown for the best glide situation. Note that the angles x and y have their smallest possible values. The best glide angle and "best glide speed" can be calculated mathematically, but the only practical way for most pilots to learn these characteristics of their glider is through actual flying.

Before we go further, we should discuss a matter that will be covered in detail in Chapter III. This is the fact that flying the airspeed that gives you the best glide ratio with respect to the air will not necessarily give you the best glide path over the ground. For example, if your glider achieves its best ratio of lift to drag (L / D max) at 23 mph, you would expect to be able to fly 23 mph and get the furthest possible distance from your take off point. However, what if you were flying in a wind that was blowing 23 mph straight at you? In this case, it is easy to see that you would sink straight down, getting nowhere. To make any headway at all, you would have to speed up. In this example, we find that to travel the most distance over the ground we have to fly faster than our "speed for best glide." In fact, the only time flying the "speed of best glide" will give you the best distance over the ground is in still air. Now still air is about as rare as a thermal at the North Pole. The air is always up to something. However, we must learn to maximize our glide ratio with respect to the air before we can learn to maximize our performance with respect to the ground in moving air.

Becoming an expert pilot is not without its demands, for to find calm air you often have to get up with the birds. The least air movement usually occurs in the early morning. Select a hill that will allow you at least 40 ft. ground clearance for the majority of the flight – the steeper the hill, the better. The object of the flight test is to fly at different speeds until you find the one that takes you the furthest from your takeoff point. If the air is not moving, then this speed should be your "best glide speed."

An airspeed indicator is very helpful in this test. Your "best glide airspeed" should be in the low 20s, so you should start at 20 mph and work your way up in 1 mph increments. (Actually, an airspeed indicator mounted at the control bar doesn't read true airspeed. This is due to a slowing of the airflow below the wing. To find out how to correct for this effect, read Chapter III.) Of course, if you already have a good idea as to what airspeed gives you your best glide, start with this and try 1 mph faster and slower. Figure 4 shows an example of flights at various airspeeds. In this case, the pilot found 23 mph to be the airspeed that took him the furthest. This is his best glide speed.

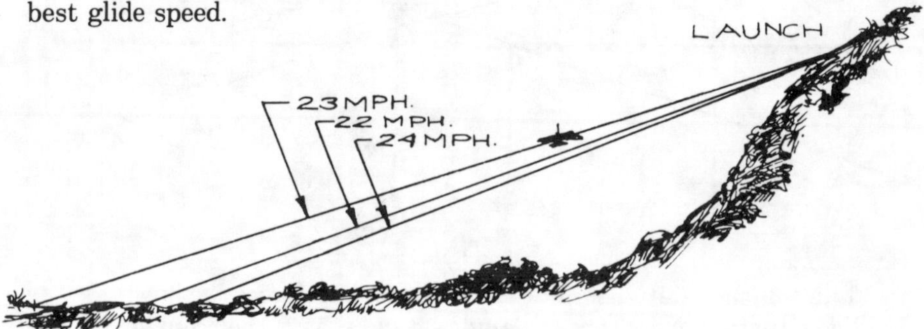

Figure 4 · Flying Best Glide Speed

If you do not have an airspeed indicator you can still perform the test. Here's how: repeat the above procedures while noting the position you are holding the control bar and the force of the wind on your face. Moving the control bar one inch forward or back corresponds to a change of about one degree in angle of attack. This is a small enough change for our test. The control bar position that takes you the furthest is your best glide position.

The majority of pilots fly without an airspeed indicator. They acquire an instinctive feel for airspeed. What this instinct really is is "muscle memory." This is what allows you to touch the tip of your nose with your eyes closed. Try it. Our eyes give us very little airspeed information – we can't see the air. Consequently we must rely on the sense of touch. Once you find the control bar position for "best glide speed," make a mental note of where your hands are in relation to your body. Also note the sound of the wind striking the glider and rushing by you. Be aware of the force of the wind on your face and the feel of the control bar. Ask yourself these questions: how much vibration do I feel? How much bar pressure is there? How quick does the glider respond? All of these items are used by advanced pilots (whether consciously or not) to judge airspeed. On a hang glider you are out in the airstream and can use your body as an indicator instead of having to rely on an instrument.

How accurate is this method of finding "best glide speed"? The answer to this question depends on how much care the pilot took in performing the test. The sources of error are: ground effect, variance of take-off technique and movement of the air. Ground effect becomes significant below heights of one wingspan (30 ft) and plays a greater role the slower you fly. Ground effect causes the glider to fly furthest at an airspeed slightly slower than its actual "best glide speed." To avoid this error fly your chosen speed as close to the ground as you can, then slow up and land as soon as possible.

When taking off, start at exactly the same place and run with the same speed. Adjust to your chosen airspeed as soon as possible to keep each flight similar. If the air is moving, accuracy will suffer, but as previously mentioned, a complete calm is seldom seen. The best policy is to duplicate the testing procedure on several occasions and take the average of the "best glide speeds" you find if they differ from test to test. Note that wing loading changes the airspeed at which stall, minimum sink and best glide occur. If you add a parachute, heavy boots, a coat or eat a big supper, the extra weight will increase the speed at which best glide occurs. A rule of thumb is: you increase all speeds by ½ mph, for every 10 lbs. of weight added. Consequently you should try to perform the tests with the same gear each time. On the other hand, no matter how you alter your flying weight, the bar position (hence angle of attack) will be the same for best glide – just the airspeed at which this occurs changes.

The next matter is one of great importance to pilots. This is how to judge your glide path while flying. From this you can learn to find your "best glide speed" in still air as well as your speed to fly for best distance when the air is moving. We shall call this the "stationary point" method.

Take a look at Figure 5(a). Here we see a glider approaching a field with a given glide angle. An X marks the spot where the pilot's flight path will bring him in contact with the ground. The pilot notices a tree, and a building somewhat closer and further than his landing spot. Sometime later he reaches the position shown in Figure 5(b). If he had observed carefully, he would have noticed a curious phenomenon. First, he would observe that the angle his landing spot makes with the horizon (angle t) does not change as he progresses down his glide path. Then he would see the angle the building makes with the horizon (angle s) gets smaller, while the angle of the tree (angle u) gets larger. Figure 6(a) shows the pilot's view of the situation in 5(a) and figure 6(b) shows his view as he progresses to the position of 5(b). Note how the distance between the objects in line with his flight path gets greater.

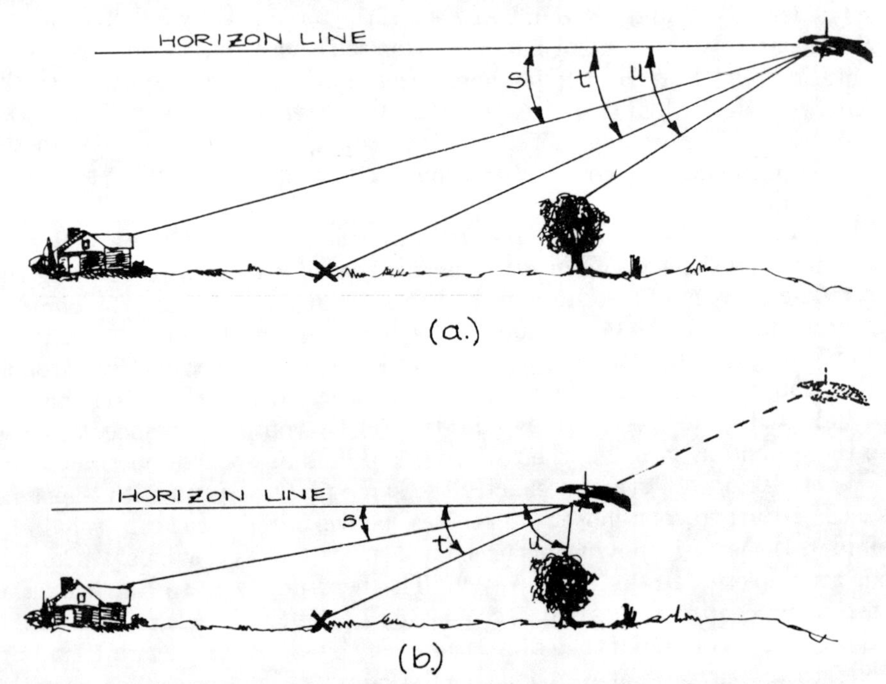

Figure 5 · Stationary Point Method

From these sketches we can make a general statement: **Any object beyond the reach of your flight path will appear to move up and away from you; any object closer to you than the point your glide path will reach will appear to move down and towards you.** An obvious and important conclusion is: **The point on the ground that is directly in line with your flight path will appear to be stationary.** This rule holds true for any glide path, including your maximum glide angle.

If you have read the above two paragraphs over carefully, you may have figured out a way to determine when you are flying at your best glide ratio (L / D max). Here's how: as you fly along at a steady speed take a few seconds to locate the point directly in front of you that appears to be growing larger, but otherwise remains stationary. This is the point to which your present glide path is directed. Now pull in on the control bar about an inch and see what happens to the point you chose. If it appears to be moving down or towards you, then your glide angle is improving (you are achieving a less steep descent). In this case, you would locate a new stationary point beyond the original one and speed up once more (pull in an inch) to see if you have yet reached your best glide.

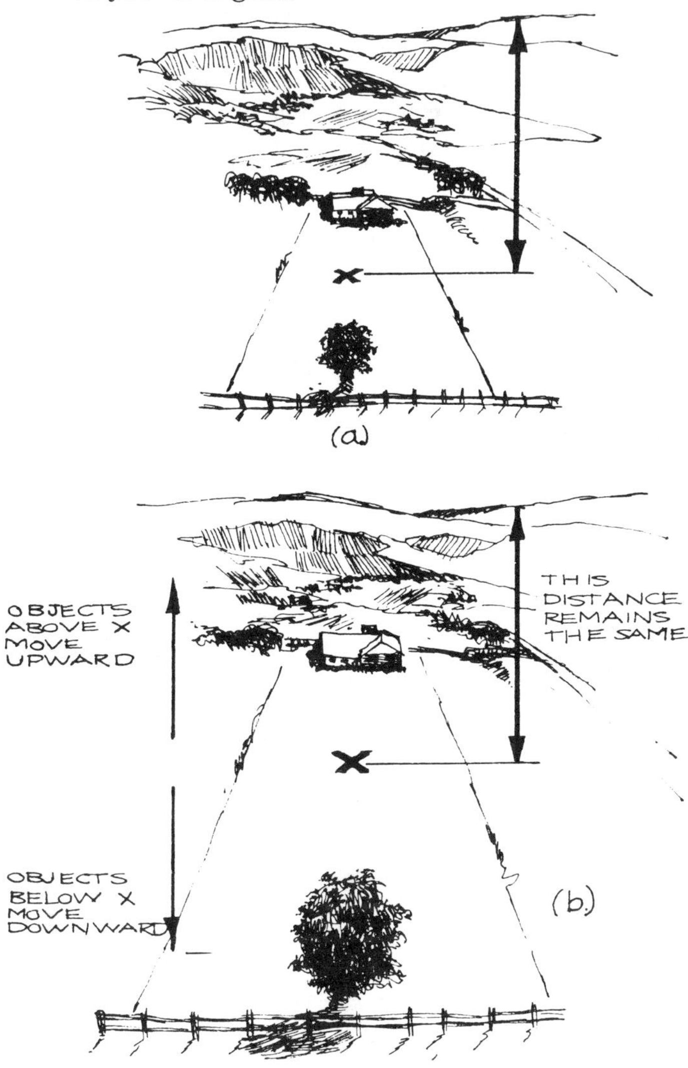

Figure 6 · Pilot's View

If the stationary point in your flight path moves up or away from you as you speed up, then your glide angle has steepened. Go back to your previous position. The same argument holds true when you slow your glider down—if the stationary point moves down towards you, your glide is improving; if the stationary point moves away from you, your glide is degrading.

This whole process may sound difficult or confusing, but the truth is, it comes easy once you try it on a few flights. In fact, many advanced pilots use this technique without really being aware of it. If you ask a pilot how he finds his "best glide speed" he may reply he "senses" it, or "feels" it. In actuality, he probably uses the method outlined above, although he can't quite put it into words.

In normal flight, you don't have to spend time looking for the "stationary point." If you locate any spot in the general area you are flying towards, you can tell if it moves toward you or away from you slower or faster. From this you can adjust your speed accordingly. For example, if a point is moving slowly toward you, then moves faster toward you as you change your speed, you have improved your glide. Similarly, if a point is moving away from you then slows down as you change your speed, you have improved your glide. The closer you are to the ground, the more accurate this method is.

A side note to this technique is the important skill of judging your clearance of ground objects. You don't have to wait till the last moment to know if your going to clear those grasping trees. Figure 7 shows how you can tell if your going to make it from a long way off. In this illustration the pilot is approaching a field located behind a power line. If he doesn't want a 10,000 volt handshake, he had better be sure that he will clear the wires. As soon as possible he locates a spot directly behind the power line. In Figure 7(a) this is shown as a dark clump of bushes. As the pilot progresses along on his flight, he keeps his eye on the bushes. If they seem to rise with respect to the power line, he will clear the wires (see 7[b]). If the bushes fall below the power line, he will not make it (see 7[c]). Of course, lift or sink will affect the outcome of both situations. However, the pilot has an excellent idea of what to expect long before it's too late to think of landing alternatives.

If we take a careful look at the "stationary point" method of detecting the best glide, we see that we really don't need to know our airspeed. Whether we are in still air, lift, sink, or headwind or a tailwind, this method will find our best glide for us. Consequently, you may ask "Why do I need to test my glider in still air to find the best glide speed?" There are two reasons for this. First, you may be too occupied or turning too much to really get a "fix" on the landscape with which to make your judgment. This is often the case in competition where you have many things to concentrate on. Secondly, if you know your "best glide speed" in still air you can begin at that speed and adjust it up or down, depending on what the air itself is doing. At this point you will be in good shape to apply the "stationary point" method. Chances are you will get by with little or no adjustment.

In Chapter III we will investigate the matter of how to adjust our still air "best glide speed" for conditions when the air is moving. The importance of learning this material as well as the "stationary point" method cannot be overemphasized. The two techniques compliment each other and should be used simulaneously. Whether you fly in competition or simply for your own self achievement, you will not get maximum performance unless you can bring out your glider's best glide. You may then save hundreds of dollars, since your old ship will start giving you the performance you thought would only come with the purchase of a new glider!

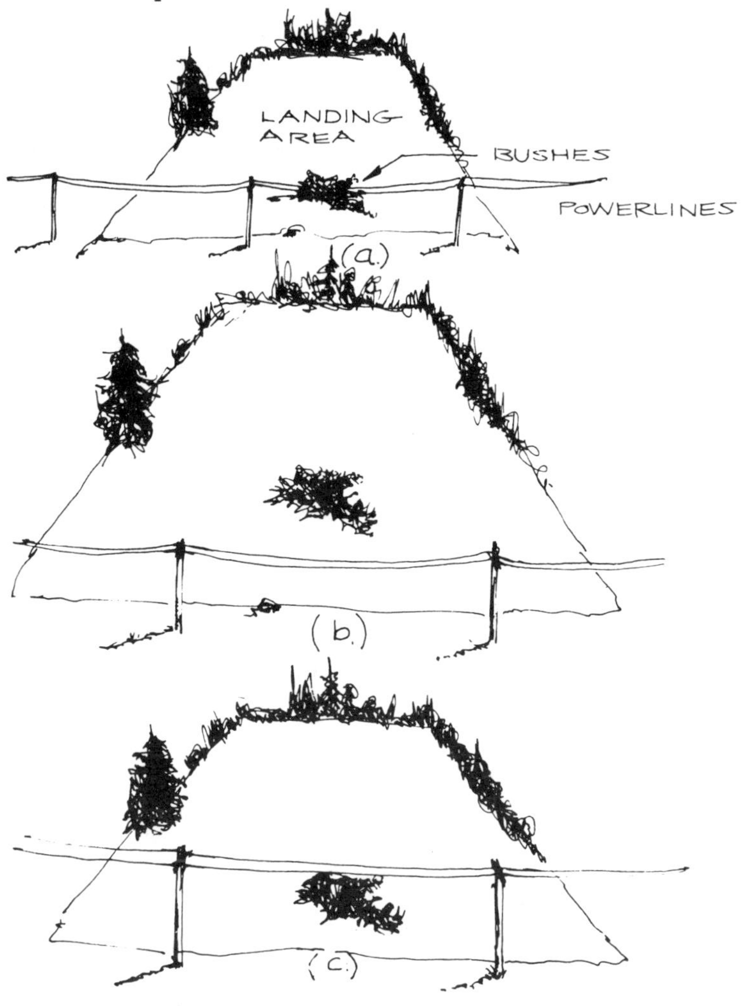

Figure 7 · Line of Sight

MINIMUM SINK SPEED

Equally as important as finding your glider's "best glide speed" is finding the "minimum sink speed." Why we want to find the airspeed that gives us our minimum sink rate is obvious – we want to stay up as long as possible. Let's take a minute and think about how a glider varies its speed and glide path as angle of attack changes.

Recall the statement made earlier: a glider's airspeed is directly related to its angle of attack – the higher the angle of attack, the slower it flies, and vice versa. In addition to the change in airspeed, the glide angle changes as the angle of attack is changed. Take a look at Figure 8. The best glide angle of attack is shown in 8(b). A lower angle of attack results in a dive as shown in 8(c). The flight velocity in each case is indicated by V. This arrow (vector) points in the direction of flight and is drawn longer for a greater speed. The vertical component of V is the arrow Vv. The horizontal component is Vh. In every case, Vv represents the rate at which the glider is falling earthward. Thus, Vv is the sink rate. Note that Vv has its smallest value in 8(a), and as such, is the minimum sink rate. We will call this value of V the "minimum sink speed." The airspeed V and the sink rate Vv is smaller at the minimum sink speed, while the glide ratio Vh / Vv is better at the best glide speed.

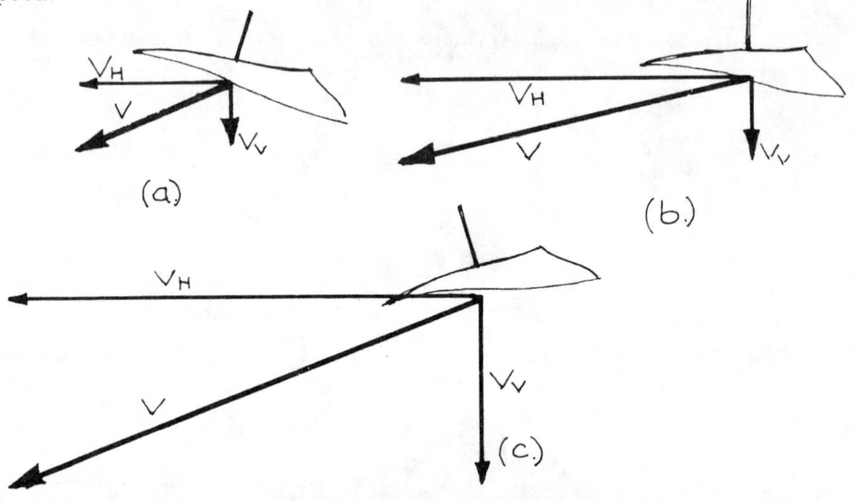

Figure 8 · Minimum Sink Rate

To be a good pilot you certainly don't need to have all these diagrams and arrows floating in your head, but you should know how your glide ratio and sink rate changes as you go from fast, low angle of attack flight to slow, high angle of attack flight. In addition, you must know at what airspeed your minimum sink occurs and you should have a good idea what your minimum sink rate is.

Finding the minimum sink speed is simple if you have a variometer. Take a high flight in mild conditions and watch the variometer dial as you gradually slow the glider from your best glide speed. You should see your sink rate diminish as you push out. Eventually you will reach the stall point and your sink rate will increase as you begin to parachute. You don't want to stall, so speed up a little until your variometer again shows the lowest sink rate. At this point, note your bar position, and airspeed either with a windmeter or through the various body signals discussed in the previous section. You have now found your "minimum sink speed."

Repeat this process several times to get an accurate feel for the exact "minimum sink speed." This is important in order to max out the lift in all types of conditions. Unlike the "best glide speed," the "minimum sink speed" doesn't change for different lift or wind conditions. The only change occurs when you add weight – about ½ mph increase for each additional 10 lbs. When you are floating around at a few thousand feet, it's nice to know you can depend on the old "minimum sink speed" to be where you left it last.

If you don't own instruments, you can still find your "minimum sink speed." The best way is to soar alongside a friend on a stable day (this means no thermals). He should be aware of your intentions and fly at a constant airspeed. You simply vary your speed while using him as a reference to see which bar position takes you highest. In ridge lift, the lower your sink rate, the higher you will top out in the lift. Of course an altimeter can be used in place of your buddy, if it is very sensitive. In addition, you can try watching a distant point, but it is hard to judge very small variations in height in this manner. Again you should repeat this test several times and carefully note your airspeed when you achieve your lowest sink rate.

Finding the minimum sink rate itself is also easy if you have a variometer. In this case you must fly in air with zero vertical movement. Repeat the slowing down procedure outlined above and read the variometer dial when it reaches its lowest value. If you fly without a variometer, you can find your minimum sink rate by flying on a calm day at your "minimum sink speed" from a hill whose height is accurately known (topographic maps help here). Time your flight from take-off to landing, then divide this time into the height of the hill and instantly you have your minimum sink rate.

The sink rate measurements are affected by vertical air movement. In addition, altitude and temperature will vary your sink rate as they affect the air density. The less dense the air is, the higher your sink rate. However, you won't notice this effect because your angle of attack and bar position is always the same for minimum sink rate. In addition, you won't notice the difference in airspeed because while you speed up in less dense air, there are fewer air molecules per unit volume. Consequently, exactly the same force of air strikes your glider, your face and your airspeed indicator. No matter what occurs, you can always fly your minimum sink rate by putting your control bar in the "minimum sink speed" position.

STALL SPEED

We cannot complete the concept of minimum sink rate without discussing the stall speed of our glider. Strictly speaking, a stall occurs when the wing of an aircraft meets the air at too high an angle of attack. The air moving over the top of a wing is forced to change its direction and wash down behind the wing. The higher the angle of attack, the greater the direction change. The air has mass and therefore, must overcome inertia effects as it changes direction. Consequently, as the angle of attack is increased, a point is reached where the air can no longer follow the upper surface of the wing. The airflow over the top becomes turbulent and unorganized, resulting in an increase in drag and a reduction in lift.

If the angle of attack is increased only a small amount above this critical point, the amount of turbulence increases rapidly. Lift is reduced considerably and drag increases dramatically. It would appear that all the pilot would have to do to recover from the stall is reduce his angle of attack a few degrees. This is not the case for the result of the loss of lift and the increase in drag is a downward acceleration and a reduction of forward speed. Both of these effects increase the angle of attack.

The final result of a hard stall in a hang glider is a sudden drop of the nose into a sharp dive. Once the glider picks up speed, lift again balances the weight and the glider returns to normal flight. Figure 9 illustrates the washout pattern of a hang glider. Washout is the amount of twist in a wing as we progress from the root (center) to the tip. From this we can see that the root of the wing is always at a higher angle of attack than any other portion. The area at the lowest angle of attack (washed out the most) is the tips.

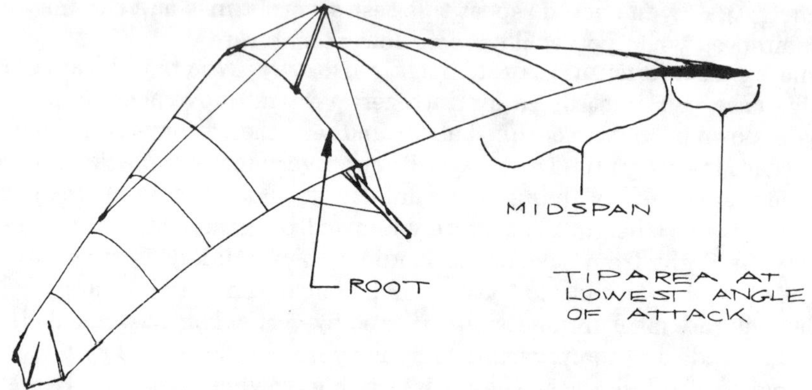

Figure 9 · Washout Patterns

Now imagine that you are flying the glider pictured, and in your mind begin pushing out on the control bar. When you reach the stall point, don't hesitate, just keep on pushing. Can you see the center section start to stall while the outer portions of the glider remain flying? This is shown in Figure 10(a). Here the stalled portion is shaded. You should be able to see that only the outer portion of the wing is producing lift. If you keep pushing the bar forward you will spread the stall further, as in 10(b). Eventually, the amount of lift will fall below that required to maintain flight, drag will increase greatly and the glider will drop is nose as in 10(c).

The cause of the dropping nose is the tenacious bit of lift remaining at the tips. This lift is behind the pilot's body and causes the rotation as his body drops. Even if the entire wing stalls, the nose drops because there is much more sail area behind the pilot than in front. The extra sail area creates extra resistance and flips the nose down as the pilot's weight is pulled earthward by gravity (see Figure 11).

In a hang glider, we have a problem defining the stall point. Different portions of the wing stall at different times, as we saw in Figure 10. We don't even talk about the angle of attack of the wing without stating which portion we are referring to. For convenience we will define the stall point of our glider as the angle of attack where the stall begins on the wing.

By defining the stall in this manner, we have pinpointed the airspeed or angle of attack where the glider changes from "flying" to "parachuting." As soon as a stall develops, the glider slows down and drops more rapidly. The parachute mode extends from the stall point to the angle of attack where the glider drops its nose—from Figure 10(a) to 10(c). Mushing or parachuting is a useful glider characteristic since it allows the pilot to vary his glide angle somewhat, as if he had airplane-type flaps. However, control is greatly reduced in such slow flight, so much caution must be exercised when flying in "mush mode" near the ground or other objects. This technique should be used by expert pilots only and then in nothing but smooth conditions.

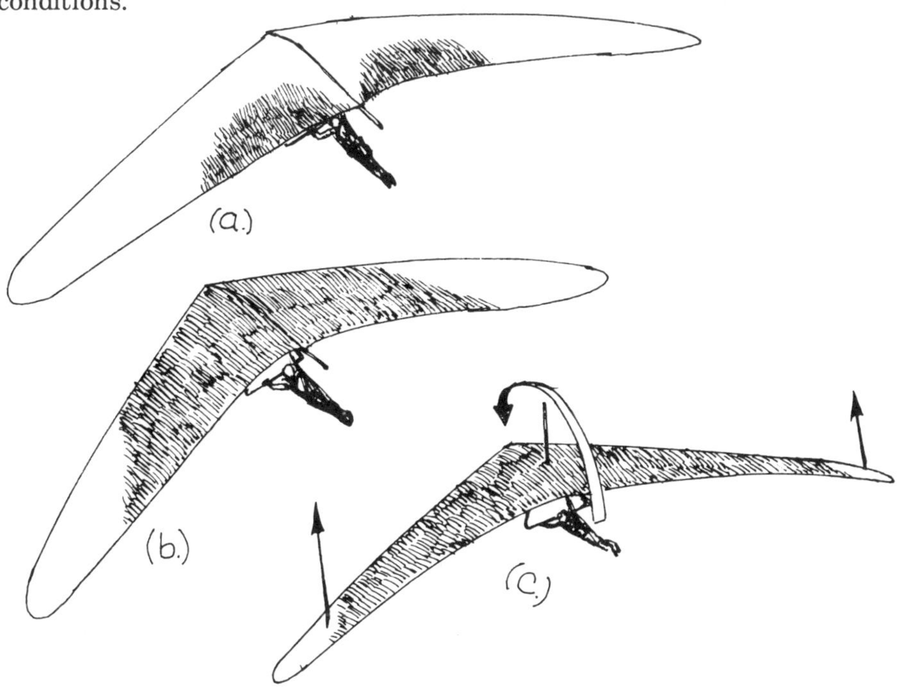

Figure 10 · Progression of a Stall

At this point we can return to the concept of "minimum sink speed." It should be clear when looking at Figure 9 that every point on the wing cannot be at the angle of attack for minimum sink. In fact, the root section reaches the minimum sink angle of attack, then begins to stall long before the outer portions are producing their maximum lift. From this we can conclude that the speed to fly to get the minimum sink rate of the glider is a fraction above the stall speed. It should be apparent that slowing up beyond the stall point will get more of the wing producing greater lift, but the loss of lift and increase in drag at the stalled root section is a greater factor and ultimately increases the sink rate.

It is a rule of thumb to fly a few miles per hour above the "stall speed" in order to achieve "minimum sink speed." The speed margin is to allow for small changes in angle of attack due to air movement. Of course, if you are flying in any condition other than the smoothest breeze, or if you want to do steep turns, you must increase your airspeed. The reason for this is simple:

any turn increases your stall speed and any turbulence varies your angle of attack randomly (this is covered in Chapter II). To put it briefly, the art of flying at minimum sink consists of flying as slow as possible without stalling.

Now the problem becomes finding the "stall speed." Of course, we can proceed in the manner outlined for finding the "minimum sink speed" and consider this to also be our "stall speed." However, the following method is more instructive and will serve as a cross check on your "minimum sink speed." Take a flight on a calm or smooth air day and progressively slow your glider (you should have at least 500 ft. ground clearance for this test).

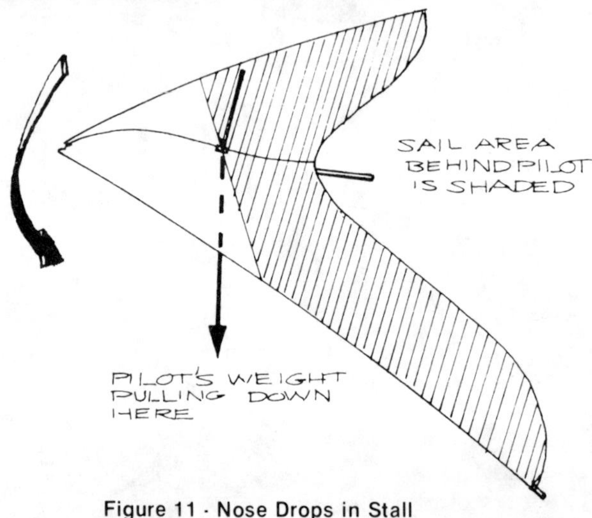

Figure 11 · Nose Drops in Stall

Eventually, you should reach the stall point. How will you recognize it? The signs are subtle but they're there. Occasionally, you may hear a buffeting in the sail, or feel a vibration through the control bar. This is caused by the turbulence created in the stalled section. A more common sign of a stall is the glider may tend to wallow or make small turns of its own accord. Each glider has its own peculiar way of announcing a stall. It is up to you to pay attention to your own glider's signals. All gliders should produce a strong back pressure on the control bar near stall, as well as feel "mushy" in roll response. Of course, you should notice a definite drop in airspeed.

You may find the exact "stall speed" is hard to pinpoint. However, that's all right because what we really want to develop is the feeling for how much maneuvering we can get away with at and below "stall speed." The real secret to slow speed flying is feeling the sluggishness of the controls. With practice you can (and should) learn exactly how your glider responds in various stall modes. To do this, simply try small side movements of the control bar as you slow down. Be sure to preserve plenty of altitude as a wing may drop if the stall moves out to the tip.

Students learning to fly an airplane get lots of practice stalling and recovering. Of course, they don't mind losing lots of altitude in a dive – they have their engine. In a hang glider we generally fly to conserve altitude.

However, it is instructive to try a full break stall with your glider at least once.

First you must be absolutely positive your craft is not divergent. Generally, the only way to know this is to see the manufacturer's proof of testing. Now, with plenty of altitude (at least 1000 ft.) push forward on the control bar until the nose drops. You will experience a sudden rapid dive. Do not jerk the control bar rapidly. This action will increase the forward rotation of the glider and cause a steeper dive. Hold the control bar out and pull it in as soon as the glider starts pulling out of the dive to avoid shooting up into another stall. This procedure will give you the ability to recover from a full-break stall whether induced intentionally or not.

When experimenting with stalls or maneuvers, avoid whipstalls at all cost. A whipstall is a stall that occurs at the end of a climb or "zoom" that results from the pull out at the end of a dive. This is shown in Figure 12. The drawing shows a glider stalling after pulling out of a dive. The problem is that the glider is at an exceedingly high attitude (nose-up position) when the stall occurs. The subsequent dive is very abrupt and steep. Note the difference in the amount of altitude required to recover from the whipstall as opposed to a stall that occurs in normal flight.

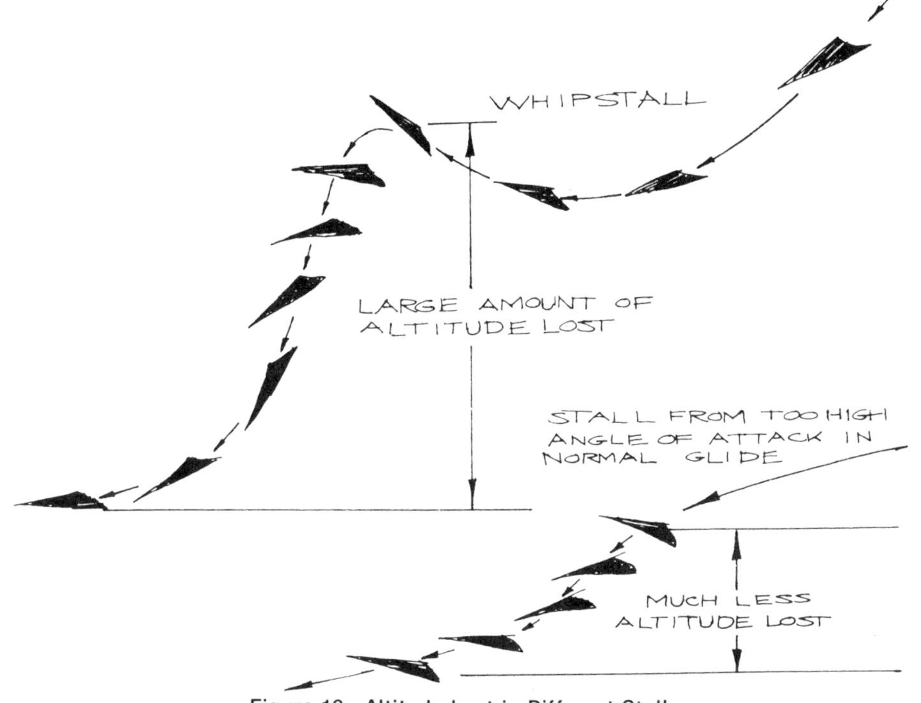

Figure 12 · Altitude Lost in Different Stalls

In a whipstall, the glider doesn't stall until it is climbing and gravity slows it down. The pilot finds he suddenly has almost zero airspeed at a high angle of attack. On the other hand, a high speed stall can occur from the same situation, with different results. When the pilot is diving fast and pushes out hard, the glider may have too much inertia to follow the intended path (see Figure 13). When this occurs, the angle of attack increases quickly to the stall angle of attack and a violent stall occurs.

The pilot caused this stall by trying to pull out of the dive too fast. Whenever a mass moves in a curved path, it experiences a force—centrifugal force. Centrifugal force increases as the radius of the curve is reduced and the velocity is increased. The extra force on the glider appears exactly as if a lot of extra weight was added (you can feel this force on a swing). In a sense, the high speed stall is beneficial. It limits the G load that the glider experiences. This was discussed on page 3.

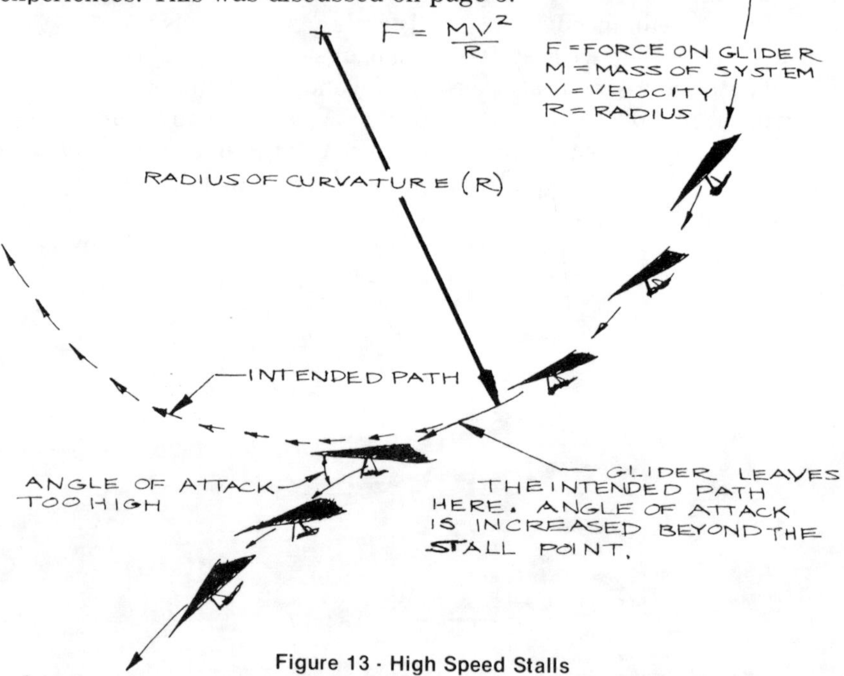

Figure 13 · High Speed Stalls

To avoid high speed stalls, a pilot simply has to avoid pushing forward on the control bar too violently when in a dive. Modern gliders with quick pitch response are more likely to enter a high speed stall than older gliders with excessive pitch damping. You would be hard put to raise the nose of a standard Rogallo fast enough to stall at high speeds.

This completes our review of a hang glider's pitch control in level flight. In turns, pitch control plays an important role, as we shall see in the next chapter. An experienced pilot should be able to use the full extent of his glider's speed range in order to maximize performance in all conditions. A little time spent in discovering our glider's specific cardinal speed positions will pay dividends in terms of rewarding flights. Again, we list them for emphasis: stall speed, min. sink speed, best glide speed and top speed.

We can't vary our speed by tucking in our wings like the birds, but then, they can't vary their speed by shifting their weight. With practice, a pilot can equal the birds on their ability to select the right speed for the occasion.

CHAPTER II

CURVING FLIGHT

After a day or two of flying, a beginner has become acquainted with pitch control and starts learning to turn. His first attempts are cautious and tentative—he is not sure what is supposed to happen. However, he gradually acquires a sense of proportion; that is, he learns how much speed he needs for how much bank and push out. Eventually he learns to perform unslipped (coordinated) turns of every bank angle. He's on his way to becoming an advanced pilot.

However, there is more to advanced turning ability than cranking and banking. A pilot must become familiar with all aspects of his glider's turning characteristics. For instance, if his glider has a noticeable adverse yaw response in a roll, he should be ready for the slight hesitation when he moves to one side of the control bar. He should also know the quickness of roll response of his glider both into the turn and out of the turn (they may be different).

In addition to knowing his glider's response in turns, a pilot should know how to vary his turns according to the conditions at hand. Its fairly easy to fly at minimum sink straight ahead, but maximizing a turn requires a bit more skill. This chapter is intended to teach a pilot the many things he must be aware of when turning.

ROLL CONTROL

Unlike pitch control, roll control has no specific position that benefits performance more than other positions. The amount of side movement the pilot extends to the control bar depends on how fast and how much he wants to bank his glider. The reason we bank our gliders is to initiate a turn or to counteract the effects of turbulence.

Moving your body to one side of the control bar creates an imbalance of forces on the glider (your weight is displaced to one side of the lifting forces). Consequently, a rotation about the lateral axis or a roll takes place. Figure 14 shows this roll control taking place with two different gliders. The top drawing shows a prone pilot (suspended above the bar) while the lower drawing represents a seated pilot. They are displaced the same distance to the side and therefore are exerting the same roll force. Note however, how the pilot with the shortest suspension (the prone pilot) must raise himself higher to achieve this side movement. The prone pilot does extra work against gravity and must exert more force when banking his glider.

In general the above situation causes no problems. If a glider is very "flexible"–that is, it has floppy tips, pliable leading edges and allows the sail to shift–there will not be much difference in the forces the two pilots exert in a turn. However, in turbulence requiring constant roll corrections the prone pilot will tire much sooner than the seated pilot. How many times have you ended a soaring flight because your arms gave out? Try suspending yourself as low as possible and see if you notice a difference.

The only advantage to suspending high off the control bar is quickness of response. With modern designs, this is not really a necessity. Various devices such as shifting billow and shifting crossbars provide all the roll response you need.

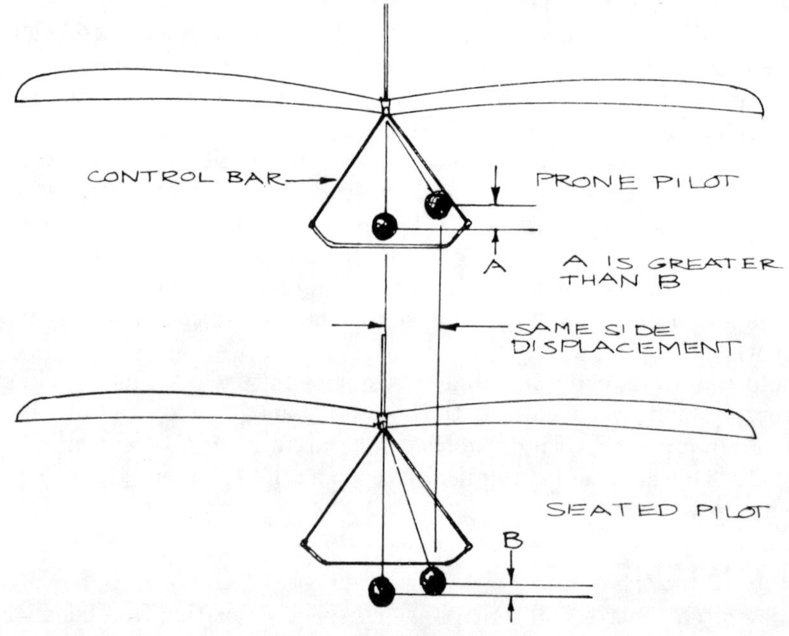

Figure 14 · Force in a Turn

THE TURN

In the preceding, we speak of roll control as an independent operation. This is rarely the case. Except for minor turbulence corrections, or very shallow bank angles, roll control is always accompanied by pitch control. The essence of a coordinated turn is combining the right amount of pushout with the amount of roll you have induced.

There has been much written on the subject of how a hang glider turns. Most of this material is an extension of that written about airplanes. Instead of repeating all the old material, we will try to look at turns from the hang gliding point of view. There are a few things that are unique to our wings. Remember, not even the birds use weight shift for control.

You may well ask, "Why do I need to read about turns, I've executed thousands of them with never a stalled wing." The answer is: there are ways to make your turns more efficient and there are many things that occur in turns that most pilots don't understand. With a little effort spent in looking at these matters, we can learn to vary our turns according to the situation at hand. New designs are continually entering the market. It pays to know what to expect in terms of their control.

Recently, a pilot bought a new high performance glider. This particular design had an adverse yaw problem. At slow speeds when the pilot moved his weight to the left, the glider yawed to the right instead of rolling left. As we shall see, this is not such a rare occurrence. If the pilot understood the dynamics of a hang glider in a turn, he would be able to cope with the adverse yaw problem. If the designer understood what was happening he could have minimized the adverse yaw problem in the glider in the first place.

Before we look at specific problems, we will review the turning process. It has been stated that "a glider turns because it is banked." This is a true statement, but to turn efficiently (that is, with a minimum loss of altitude) we must add some pitch control. To suit our purposes here though, we will separate a turn into two steps: first a roll action to set up the desired bank angle, then a pitch control (push forward) to eliminate slipping and "carve" the turn.

Looking at the second step of our turn first, we imagine a glider rolled into a steep bank as shown in Figure 15(a). The glider is going away from us so it is banked left to turn left. Gravity is pulling the weight (W) of the pilot and glider downward. The only other force involved is the resultant force (R) due to the drag and lift the glider creates. The combination of the two forces (R and W) results in a force (S) pulling the glider down and to the side. At this point, the glider is in a sideslip. If the glider is directionally stable (most hang gliders are), the glider will yaw to the left, due to the greater drag on the left side. This yawing action is shown in 15(b), which is a side view of the banked glider.

Since the glider is banked this yawing action also lowers the nose or reduces the angle of attack (try this with a model) and the glider speeds up. However, before the nose drops too much, the pilot pushes forward on the control bar. This action starts the turn and the glider follows the spiral path shown in 15(b). The reason the glider follows a spiral path instead of carving a neat circle is that it must fall through the air to create forward motion and lift. An airplane can circle by virtue of its roaring engine, but not the simple hang glider.

Once the pilot pushes forward on the control bar, another apparent force arises due to the curving path. This is centrifugal force which builds up to exactly equal the amount of inward force the resultant (R) imparts to the glider (see Figure 15[c]). The centrifugal force acts on the pilot's body and pulls him back to the center of the control bar. The apparent weight of the pilot (and glider) has increased due to centrifugal force, so even though the pilot pushes out to a high angle of attack, the glider still maintains good speed. In fact, the glider moves fast enough to build up the resultant force to equal the increased weight. Thus, we have a completely balanced situation which produces a continuous turn as long as the pilot maintains his push out.

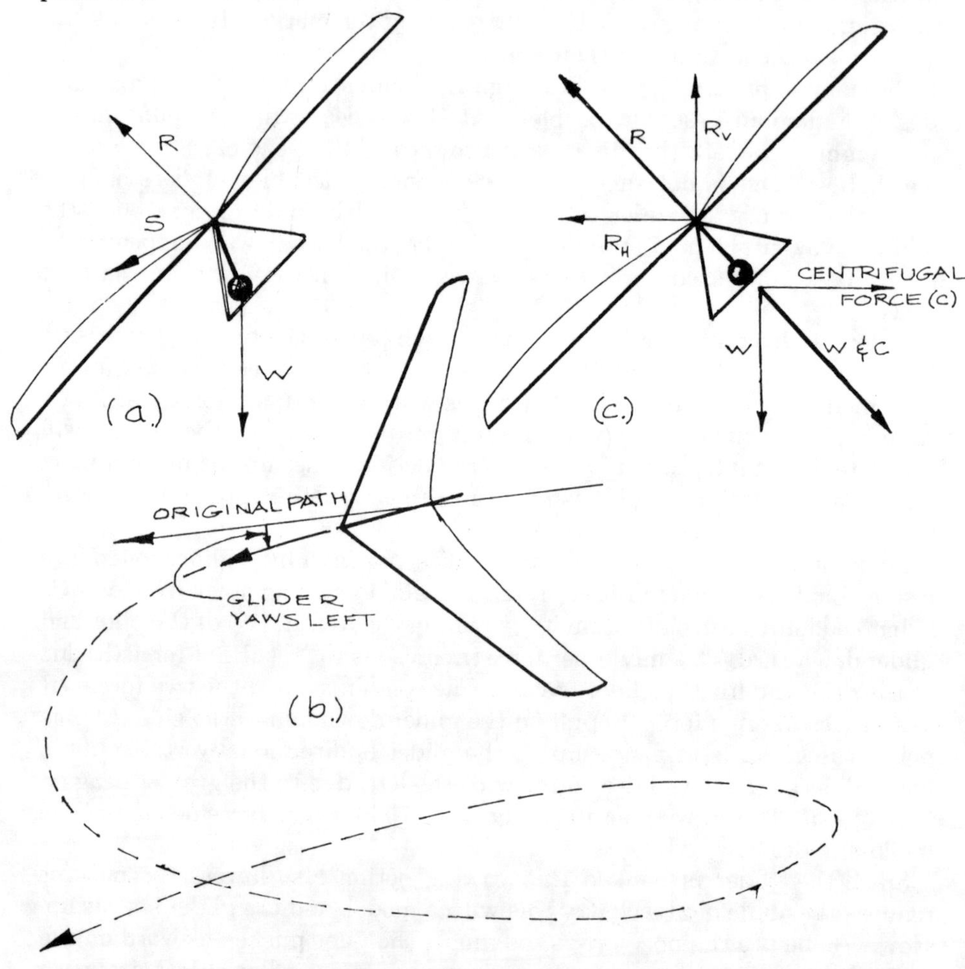

Figure 15 · Yawing in a Turn

The turn we have just described is like a dance step learned from footprints painted on the floor – not too smooth. In actuality, roll and pitch control are induced simultaneously. As soon as you start to roll, you start pushing out. To look at the situation another way, imagine that instead of one large roll followed by a large pitch control, the pilot performed a series of small roll then pitch controls to get to the turn position of Figure 15(c). It's like climbing the roll-pitch stairs. Now, make the steps smaller and smaller, at the same time increasing their number and you'll arrive at a continuous roll and pitch control motion. The secret of a good turn is maintaining the right amount of push out along with the amount of roll you produce.

How much is the right amount of push out? This is something no one can tell you (except perhaps some wizened old seagull on a windswept beach), for it varies with every glider, every pilot and every angle of bank. However, once we clear up a few concepts, you can easily find out yourself.

First, let's see why you must push out in a turn. A glider banked to the left as in Figure 15(a) has an unbalanced force to the left. However, this force merely wants to pull the glider to the left and down, not actually turn it. If the pilot held this position, he would find himself in a steep diving sideslip. The glider would slowly yaw to the left, which is a turn of sorts, but a very inefficient one.

Now let's assume the glider has an excess of speed. When the pilot pushes out, he starts a curving flight path. This is true whether he is banked or not. The sequence of events shown in Figure 16 explains why the flight path curves. In 16(a) the pilot is in straight and level flight with a good supply of speed. The upward forces balance the downward forces exactly. Now he begins to push out as in 16(b). His weight is displaced behind the upward force so that the nose rotates upward. This increase in angle of attack has two effects: the upward force is increased and its location moves back due to the increase of lift on the wing tips (in fast flight the tips of a hang glider do much less lifting than the root section since they are at a much lower angle of attack). The rotation of the glider and the rearward shift of the upward force realign the forces as in 16(c). Now, however, the upward force is greater than the downward force and the glider accelerates upward. This upward acceleration increases the apparent weight due to centrifugal force until all forces are again in balance as in 16(d).

The upward curving flight would continue as long as the pilot held the bar out except for one thing. A glider rises, it does work against gravity, loses energy and slows down. Consequently the upward force is reduced and the glider will stall if the pilot doesn't pull the bar in somewhat. On the other hand, in a turn, the force turning the glider is directed inward. The same sequence of events take place as described, but the pilot has rolled the glider along with his push out so that the curving flight takes place to the left or right instead of upward. Thus, the work against gravity does not take place and the curving flight can be maintained as long as the pilot wills it.

This elaborate discussion explains what happens, but the pilot still doesn't know how much to push out. Be patient – we still have to determine how much speed we need in a turn. The minimum amount of speed needed for a turn depends on the bank angle. This is easy enough to determine if we know the stall speed of the glider in straight and level flight. In a turn, the apparent weight of the pilot is increased, so the stall speed increases just as if a heavier pilot were flying the glider. If your glider stalls at 18 mph, for example, in straight and level flight it would stall at 19.3 mph in a 30° bank, 21.4 mph in a 45° bank and 25.5 mph in a 60° bank.

Now, the speed to fly for minimum altitude loss is the minimum sink speed. This speed being so near the stall speed is also about the slowest you can fly, so the radius of your turn will also be at a minimum. Flying at your minimum sink speed produces the most efficient turn, so there's no reason to use any other airspeed. So you say, "if I want to perform a 45° banked turn all I have to do is speed up to 22 mph (add ad bit to the stall speed for control), roll to a 45° bank and hold the same amount of pitch." Unfortunately, you would be wrong. The truth is, the bar position for a given speed in straight and level flight has nothing to do with the bar position for the same airspeed in a turn. In fact, making the glider fly at a given angle of attack and thus airspeed, requires a greater amount of push-out as well as a harder push-out force for larger angles of bank.

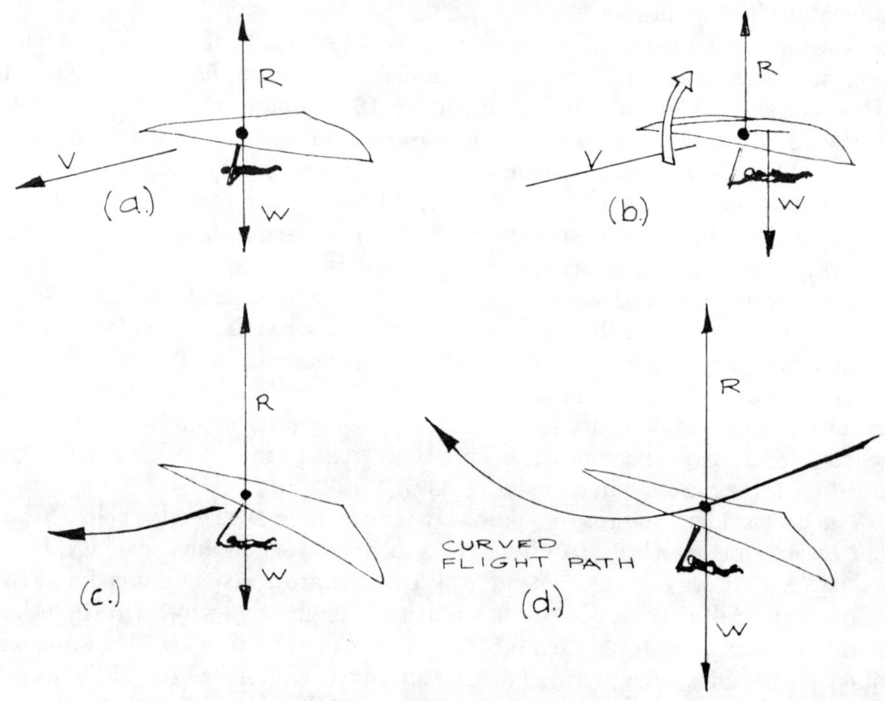

Figure 16 · Forces in Curving Flight

This may be a startling revelation to some readers, but if you think about it you will remember experiencing the hard push forces with your arms fully extended in a high bank turn. To further your understanding, imagine a pilot in a continuous steep turn as in Figure 17. This is a common situation requiring a lot of forward push as shown. Now imagine that the pilot simply rolls out of the turn but holds the same amount of pitch. What happens? He stalls like a pigeon with a spastic tail, of course. The push-out that was proper for the steep turn is far too much for straight flight.

What is the reason for the extra force and distance of forward push needed in a turn? Look at Figure 18. Here we see a glider in a left turn with arrows indicating the motion of different points on the glider. An arrow is drawn straight down at both tips and the nose. This represents the sink rate, which is equal at each point since the glider keeps the same bank angle. The arrows pointing straight ahead represent the horizontal velocity of each point. We see that the inside wingtip is moving the slowest, while the outside wingtip moves the fastest. (This is logical, since points on any rotating object move faster the further they are from the center of rotation.) The double arrows show the actual motion of each point on the glider (the combination of the horizontal and vertical velocity). Since the wind the glider "feels" is exactly opposite to the direction of travel, we can draw several conclusions.

Figure 17 · Push Out in a Steep Turn

First, the velocity of the outside tip is greater, while its angle of attack is somewhat smaller than any other point on the glider. Secondly, the inside (left) tip is moving the slowest but has a much greater angle of attack than any other point. Finally, the amount of push out will be limited by the inside wing since a stall will occur here first.

The result of the first two observations is that the tips are working much harder in a turn than they do in level flight. You can see the tips wash out a great amount in a turn. This means the total upward force lifting the glider moves back considerably and a pilot has to push himself back much further to keep the nose up. One of the reasons you have to push harder is simply that you must displace your body further. Another reason is that you are increasing your apparent weight through centrifugal force. In a 60° turn you have to push back twice as much weight! You had better start developing your triceps for those high bank turns.

The conclusion we draw from the final observation is that we can't quite slow down in a turn as much as we thought. This is because the stall speed we calculated for different angles of bank was for the root (center) section since this is where the stall occurs in level flight. In a turn, the inside wing stalls before the root so we have to maintain a bit more speed. Of course, tip washout helps reduce this increase in speed.

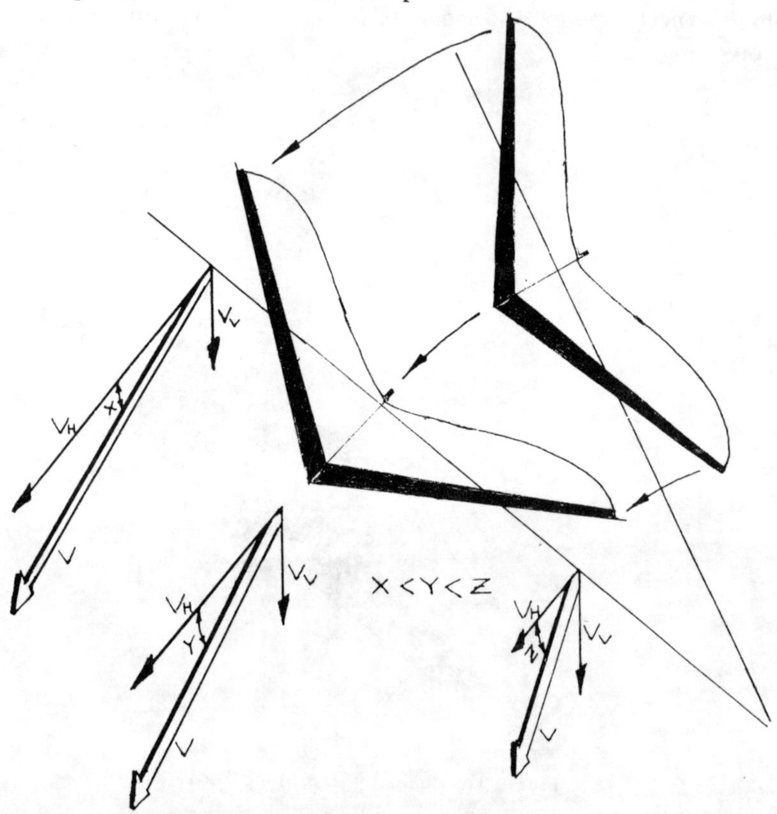

Figure 18 · Variation of Speed in a Turn

Now we can answer both how much speed and how much push-out we need in a turn. Simply push out and slow up until just before the inside wing stalls. This sounds ambiguous, but in actual practice this is what a pilot does. When you have reached the proper amount of push-out for a co-ordinated turn, the glider will maintain a steady speed throughout the turn. If you have pushed out too much, it will gradually slow and the inside tip will stall. If you have pushed out too little, the glider will gain speed and begin slipping.

There is no shortcut to knowing your glider's turning characteristics. You have to experiment. When you approach the stall point the inside tip may retard as if it were hooked by an invisible wire. If your glider has fixed tips, you may find yourself in a flat spin (these maneuvers are discussed later in this chapter) if you stall a tip, so carry out your fine line experimentation at altitude. Another sign of an impending stall is a loss of airspeed—everything suddenly seems so quiet.

If you are alert and sensitive you will be able to feel your glider's angle of attack limit for every angle of bank. A piece of yarn tied where you can see it will indicate if you are slipping or not. If the yarn points to one side instead of straight back, you are slipping. If you are slipping, you aren't pushed out enough.

You can correct your pitch control mistakes in the following manner: if you feel you are going too slow (that is, you are pushed out too far) you can either pull in a little (quickly) **or** increase your angle of bank. Think about this a minute. Increasing your angle of bank actually lowers your angle of attack (you slip and yaw a bit) so that your too slow speed becomes just right. Increasing the bank will create a tighter turn, while pulling in will allow you to continue on the same path. Take your choice. Both methods will use up about the same amount of altitude to complete the turn.

Now what do you do if you are going too fast? Naturally you would be slipping and you push out, **or** you can roll out a bit (reduce your bank angle). Rolling out of the turn increases your angle of attack so the glider adjusts happily to the excessive amount of speed. In this case you roll out if you want to increase the radius of your turn and push out if you want to continue the same turn radius.

When you enter a turn you need enough speed to keep above the stall point. If you are flying near stall speed, you should pull in a bit before you start your turn. Once you start your roll control, you can begin pushing out. The roll and push-out continues until you reach the bank angle you desire. Then you stop increasing the roll but continue the push-out until you are flying just above the stall point. To roll out of the turn, simply reverse the procedure. Of course, you must pull in as you reduce the amount of bank.

An alternate method of entering a turn is to start a roll without pulling in. This will start a slight slip and gain you airspeed. You can then start your push-out. With this method your push-out is just a bit behind your roll so that the glider slips until the roll stops while the push-out continues. This method is inefficient for several reasons. First, the turn will be sluggish (you are partially depending on the glider to yaw you around). If you pull in before you roll, the extra speed will help snap you into the turn. Secondly, the slipping loses extra altitude. Finally, you cannot roll without stalling a wing if you are flying close to stall speed in many gliders. The reason for this is the wing that is lowered by the rolling action has its angle of attack increased by the downward movement.

The amount of pull-in before the roll increases as the steepness of the intended turn increases. If you pull in too much, don't worry, you'll gain altitude as you push out in the turn. Eventually you should learn how much pull-in precedes each angle of bank. Of course, this varies with your flying speed. If you are already flying fast you may not have to pull in at all.

As you can see from the preceding material, there are many variables that require pilot judgment in a turn. Most experienced pilots will be making these judgments automatically. Indeed, the ability to react automatically to every flight situation is one of the qualities of an advanced pilot. However, it pays to review the flying process every so often and inspect one's control movements. Chances are you have fallen into the sloppy habit of slipping or some equally inefficient form of turning. Use your understanding of turns to improve the general quality of your flying.

THE YAW

In the preceding section we covered the pilot's input in a turn. Here we will investigate the glider's contribution and look at a method of varying our turns. A hang glider has a unique method of control – that is, by weight shift. In addition, the flexible wing surface creates conditions not found in any other aircraft. We want to keep these two facts in mind as we proceed with our investigation.

Let's start with our pilot flying straight and level. He pulls in a bit then shifts his weight to the left side of the control bar. What really happens? For one thing he has increased the load on the left wing and decreased the load on the right. How does a wing react when you increase the wing loading? It speeds up, right? That's exactly what happens. This is shown in Figure 19. The pilot, intending to perform a left turn shifts his weight to the left and the left wing moves down and forward. In essence, the glider has yawed to the right – the opposite direction we want it to yaw for a left turn. This yawing in the wrong direction is termed "adverse yaw" and appears in

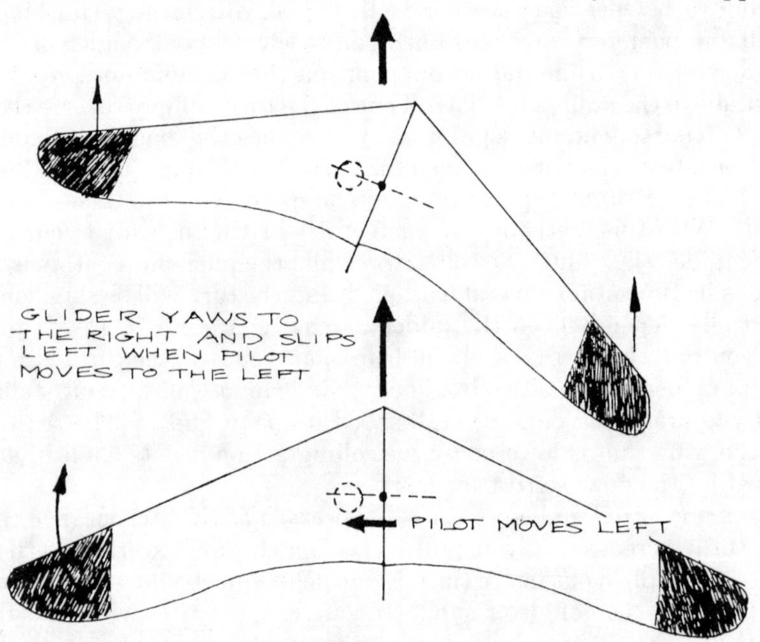

Figure 19 - Adverse Yaw

all aircraft.

In an airplane, adverse yaw is caused by the drag on the ailerons. The ailerons are flipper-like attachments on the wing which change its angle of attack. The aileron on the right wing goes down to produce more lift and roll left. This downward deflection also creates more drag so that the right wing falls behind the left wing, which again, is adverse yaw.

An airplane pilot controls adverse yaw by using a rudder in a turn. In addition, modern aileron designs incorporate low drag features. A hang glider (usually) has no rudder. Consequently all hang gliders exhibit adverse yaw. Usually the effect is unnoticeable due to the relatively large amount of sweep in most hang gliders. However, newer designs with wide nose angles (120° or more) do yaw adversely under certain conditions. Every pilot should understand these conditions and use adverse yaw to their advantage.

Most modern hang gliders have ailerons. "What?" you say, "There's no flippers on my wing tips." Oh, but there is, and these "ailerons" contribute important causes of adverse yaw. The ailerons you have are a result of billow shift. Billow shift has been around since the beginning of hang gliding (the keel of standards used to bend to give one side a bit more billow), but it wasn't really noticed until the introduction of the stand-up keel pocket in 1976.

Figure 20 shows the action of billow shift. As the pilot moves to the left of the control bar to start a left turn, the load on the left side of the sail becomes greater than that on the right. This causes the sail to shift to the left as the left wing moves down. Note how the sail is loosened or "billowed" on the left and tightened on the right.

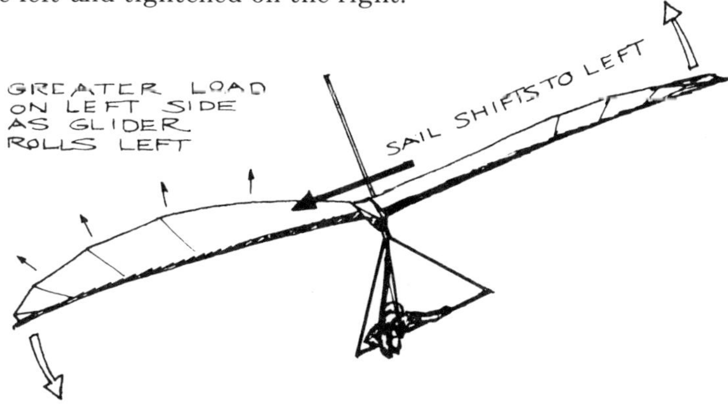

Figure 20 · Billow Shift

The result of this billow shift is a change in angle of attack on both sides of the wing. The sail washes out more on the left and greatly reduces the angle of attack. On the right, the angle of attack is increased, especially out at the tip. This change in angle of attack affects the glider exactly as if ailerons were used. The right wing creates more lift, while lift is reduced on the left. Thus, the glider wants to roll fast – much faster than without billow shift. Unfortunately, the right wing also produces more drag than the left (whenever you produce more lift, you pay a drag penalty). Thus, we have a case of airplane-type adverse yaw.

Billow shift enhances adverse yaw caused by weight shift. Whenever you force a wing downward, you tilt the lifting forces forward. This is what accelerates you forward when you increase wing loading. Figure 21(a) shows an airfoil in a normal glide. Lift (L) and drag (D) are combined to form the upward force (R). If we force this airfoil down by adding weight, we increase the angle of attack since the airfoil "sees" a greater upward component of relative wind. This is an entirely different situation than if we increase the angle of attack by tilting the airfoil. If we move the airfoil down, the upward force (R) has a forward component as in 21(b). This forward component accelerates the glider forward until the original angle of attack is established at a higher velocity.

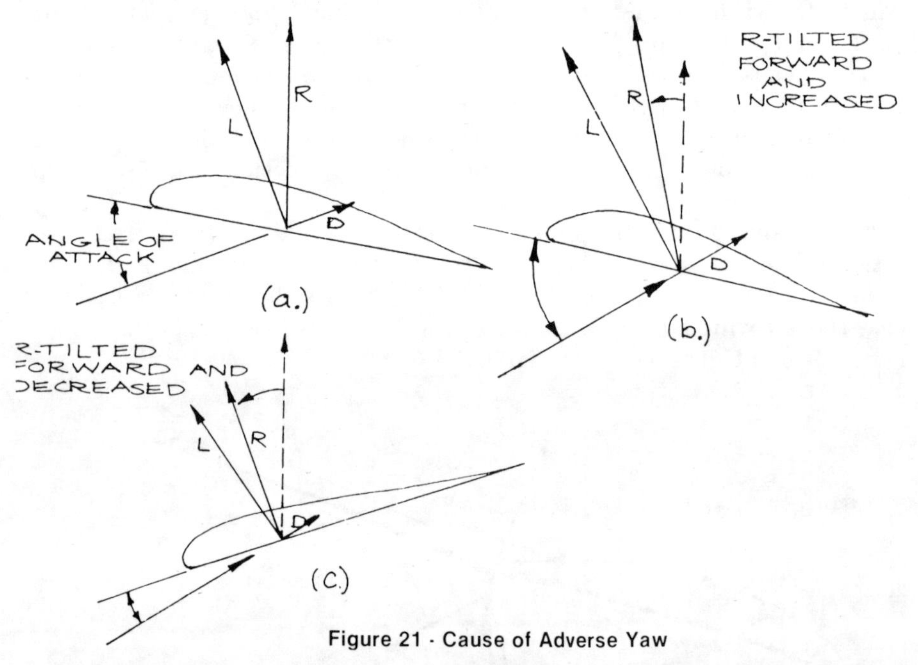

Figure 21 · Cause of Adverse Yaw

If a glider employs billow shift, the situation is changed to that shown in Figure 21(c). As the billow shifts toward the downward moving wing, more washout occurs and the angle of attack is lowered as the airfoil or sail tilts forward. Note how the force R is angled forward much more than in 21(b), indicating a greater forward component.

Since the forward component of the upward force is one of the causes of adverse yaw when we shift our weight, it should be obvious that billow shift makes it worse. Another factor that comes into play is flying speed. By now you should be aware that adverse yaw is caused by a different angle of attack on each wing, which in turn causes a difference of drag. The total drag varies more for a given change in angle of attack at low speeds. (This is because induced drag is more susceptible to changes in angle of attack than parasitic drag. Induced drag occurs at low speeds.) Thus, adverse yaw effects are greater the slower you are flying. This is the important point to remember.

Now that we have some insight into the adverse yaw problem, let's continue with our left turn and observe the glider's reaction. When we last left our pilot, he was on the left side of the control bar and his left wing had moved down and forward. The adverse yaw represents a slip to the left. As can be seen in Figure 22, he relative wind striking the glider is from the pilot's left. In addition, banking the glider to the left results in a left slip.

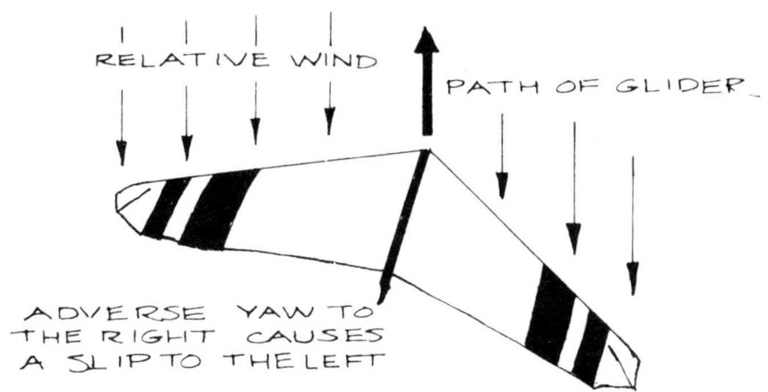

Figure 22 · Slipping Due to Yaw

As a result of the left slip, powerful forces are set up to yaw the glider to the left. Yawing to the left is what we want the glider to do, so now we are on the right track. The reason the glider yaws left when a left slip occurs is shown in Figure 23(a). This is a view looking at the glider as the air "sees" it. We are stationed a little below and to the left of the glider. The more we see of the sail, the greater the angle of attack is on that portion.

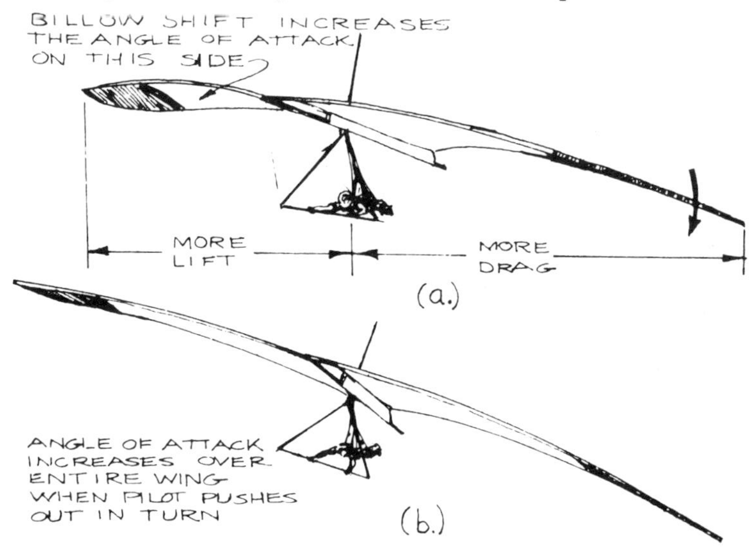

Figure 23 · Yawing Due to Slip

From the drawing we can see that the left wing is facing the relative wind much more than the right wing. The drag on the left side is greater than on the right. Thus, the left wing falls back and a yaw to the left is the result. When this left yaw action starts, the right wing starts moving faster (it is now on the outside of the turn). The fast moving right wing develops more and more lift and helps roll the glider. Billow shift helps this action by increasing the angle of attack on the right side.

When the glider begins yawing to the left, the pilot should begin pushing out. This increases the angle of attack of the whole wing. Figure 23(b) shows the relative wind "view" after the glider has yawed left somewhat and the pilot has pushed out.

When the pilot reaches his desired angle of attack, he centers his body so that the load is equalized on both sides of the wing. This equalizes the billow and the glider continues in a stable turn as described earlier. Of course, once again the action of all the forces occurs in a continuous manner, not in steps. As soon as the adverse yaw starts, the left slip starts building the left yaw forces until they overpower the adverse yaw forces. At the same time the glider is continuing its left roll. The amount of adverse yaw depends on glider design (this is the subject of Chapter V), as well as flying speed. If a glider has a definite adverse yaw problem, the pilot should be sure to pull in when flying very slow before making a turn.

Now let's look at a way of using adverse yaw to our benefit. Imagine yourself working marginal ridge lift or very light thermals. At some point you have to perform a turn. Turns cause a greater loss of altitude so you want to perform the turn efficiently. The sequence in Figure 24 shows how to avoid speeding up yet not suffer from adverse yaw.

Assume you want to do a left turn. The first thing you do is rotate your body to the right (see 24[a]). Since your body's rotational inertia is about six tenths that of the glider, the glider will yaw a bit to the right (24[b]). As soon as the glider starts to yaw back to the left, pull your body to the left side of the bar (24[c]) at the same time rotate your body all the way to the left (24[d]). Now complete the turn as you normally would.

This complicated sounding action can actually be done in one fluid motion. Practice it hanging in your garage or basement. It will allow you to perform a turn at minimum sink speed with a minimum loss of altitude. In addition, it will speed up the roll of a slow reacting glider.

Essentially, this method works by eliminating the roll induced left slip. The left slip is the mechanism that starts the necessary left yaw. However, with the above method the left yaw is aided by the pilot's energetic body rotation. Learn to perfect this technique for those "scratching for lift days."

In general, all turns must be accompanied by a yaw input. The reason for this is that our arms are a few feet ahead of our body's center of gravity or main suspension point. If we just move our arms to one side when making a control, our body will rotate around its center of gravity (just below the waist), causing no real weight shift. To move our weight to one side, then, we must push forward with the arm on the outside of the intended turn (right arm for a left turn, left arm for a right turn). At the same time, the opposite arm is holding in and moving the upper body in the direction of the turn. Try this action on a suspended control bar or when you are doing a hanging harness check.

The important matter to learn from all this is that the amount of yaw input can be varied for any given amount of weight shift. For example, you can move your body to the left one foot keeping your body parallel to the keel, or you can angle your body with respect to the keel, still keeping the total weight shift the same. It all depends on the arm positions and pressures. Practice varying turn controls in this manner.

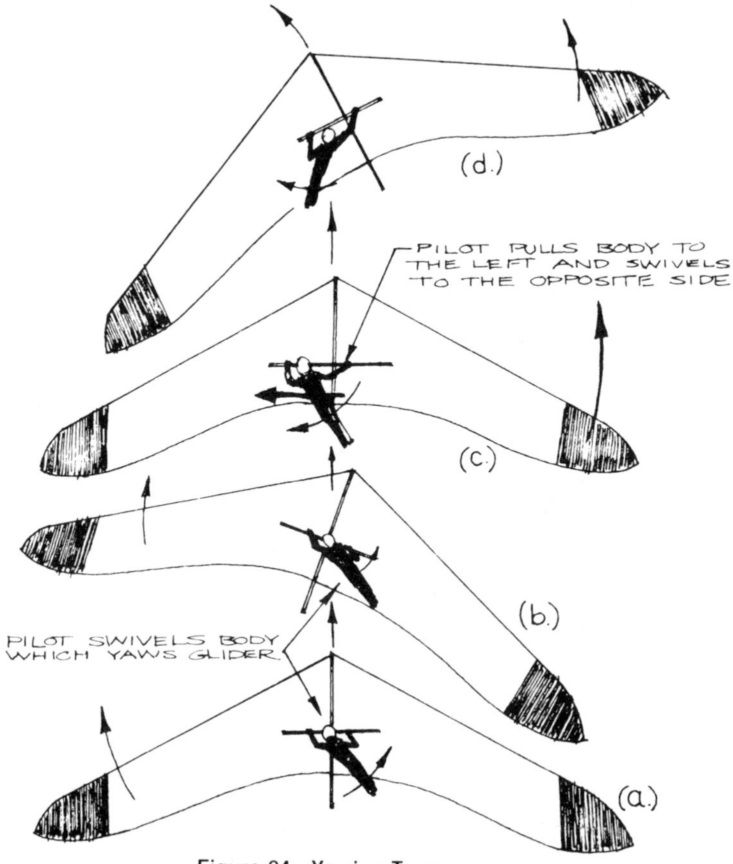

Figure 24 · Yawing Turns

Different gliders will turn best using various amounts of yaw input. A wide-nosed glider (with low yaw damping) will usually require more yaw input for most efficient performance. Experiment with your glider to find the best control combination.

THE LIMITS OF A TURN

We now have the understanding needed to perfect our turns and use them to maximum advantage. At this point we should determine what the limits are to our turning ability.

We have already seen that flying too slow for a given bank angle will result in a stall. The reason for this is all speeds increase as the wing loading increases. In a turn, the wing loading increases as the bank angle increases. Thus, it is entirely possible to be flying a speed that would be below the stall speed as soon as you banked the glider.

What happens when a glider stalls in a turn? As noted previously, the inside wing stalls first (it is moving slowest and is at the highest angle of attack). This usually results in a dropping inside wing. In fixed wing or older model gliders, a spin may result. Figure 25 shows the result of a spin. The pilot pushed out too far while turning left and stalled the left wing (25[a]). Due to the stall, the drag is suddenly increased while the lift is reduced. This retards the left side while allowing the right wing to swing around (25[b]). The bank angle will steepen and the glider will continue turning within a small radius.

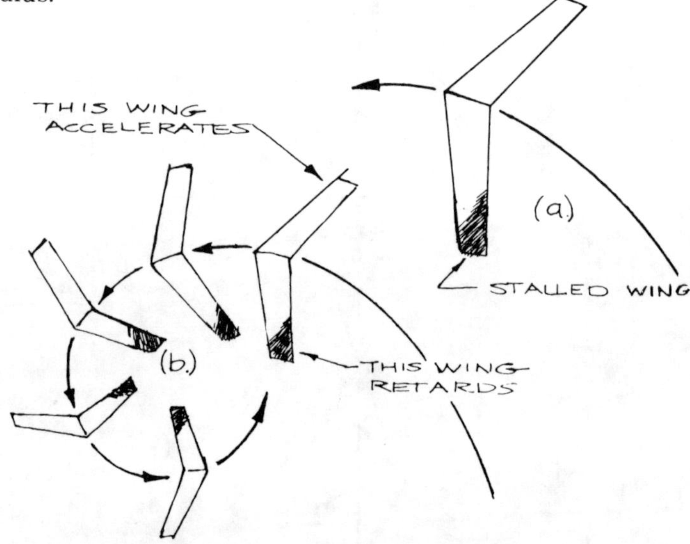

Figure 25 · Top View of a Spin

The pilot has very little control over the glider in a spin. If a pilot tries to recover from a spin by unbanking the glider he actually makes it worse. The reason for this is shown in Figure 26. In 26(a) the pilot has entered a spin. The glider starts to bank more and he tries to recover control by moving to the high side of the bar (to the right). This loads the right side up more which in turn shifts the billow to the right (26[b]). Now the sail on the left side has been tightened. This effectively increases the angle of attack on the left side which **worsens** the stall which **worsens** the spin.

The proper spin recovery is shown in Figure 26(c). Here the pilot moves to the stalled side of the glider and pulls in. This will shift the billow to the stalled side and speed the glider up. Both result in a lower angle of attack

85545

and an unstalling of the tip. If a spin occurs near the ground, you may not have a chance to dip the wing and speed up. In this case, climb the high side of the bar to reduce the airspeed of the glider. You will kick up some dust, but chances are you won't get hurt since the descent rate can be quite low in a spin.

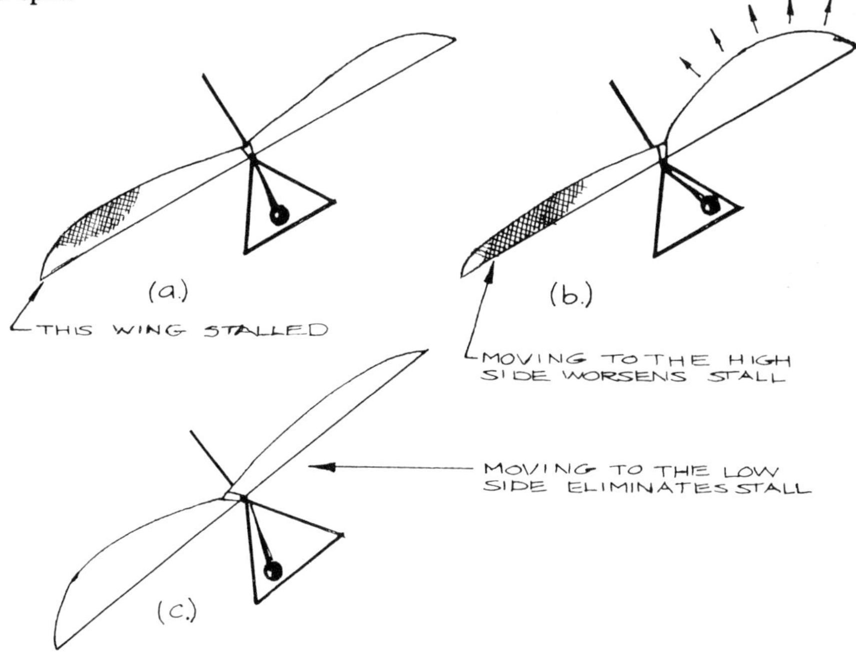

Figure 26 · Spin Recovery

You will recognize a stalled wing by the sudden slowing of this wing. Learn to react immediately to this condition by moving to the low end of the control bar. The glider will slip a little, turn the nose toward the low side and speed up. When you feel the stalled wing "free itself," you can then reduce the bank and push out to slow up.

Fortunately, most hang gliders are very spin resistant. However, a stalled wing tip is quite common near the ground. The reason for this is the reduction of tip vortices by the presence of the ground. Tip vortices are caused by air flowing towards the tip of the glider and swirling up at the end. Within a wingspan of the ground the vortices are reduced 5 percent, falling to 40 percent when the glider is at the height of a chord. The result of reducing the tip vortices is to effectively increase the angle of attack – mostly at the tip. Thus, the closer we fly to the ground, the easier it is to stall a tip. The remedy is to maintain a little extra speed when landing and avoid rolling the glider close to the deck.

We have seen the result of flying too slow in a turn, now we turn our attention to what happens if we fly too fast. We saw before that curving flight increases the load on the glider. In fact, in a coordinated 90 ° banked turn, the load would have to be infinite. Obviously this is an impossibility. What real-

YANKTON COMMUNITY LIBRARY
YANKTON, SOUTH DAKOTA 57078

ly happens in an exceedingly high bank turn is the inertia of the glider doesn't allow it to follow the necessary turn path so the angle of attack is increased and it stalls. This is the same sort of high speed stall that occurs if you suddenly push out to pull out of a dive.

A hang glider doesn't usually have the problem of high speed stalls due to their low top speed and pitch damping. However, in a steep slip, you can push out fast enough to stall the glider despite an abundance of airspeed. Avoid high speed slips near the ground and you will have no problem with this potentially dangerous form of stall.

With the knowledge we now have we can talk about the "best" turn. Usually, a coordinated (non-slipping) turn is best, but at what bank angle? There are several general cases. First, if you are required to turn at a certain point (e.g., a pylon in competition) you want the turn which will lose you the least altitude. A slow wide turn will reduce your sink rate, but will require too much time to complete, thus losing more altitude ultimately. A quick, steep turn drops you too fast. Your best bet is to turn as slow as you can at a 45° bank. This coordinated 45° bank turn will produce the least amount of altitude loss for any given amount of change in heading. For example, if we wish to perform two 360s over a pylon and minimize our altitude loss, we must maintain a bank of 45°. A shallower bank loses more altitude due to the extra time required; a steeper bank loses more altitude due to the much greater sink rate.

On the other hand, if you are in widespread lift or merely floating, around and there's no need to hurry the turn, the lowest bank, slowest flying turn you can manage is best. If, for instance, you are in very light ridge lift or in no lift at all and want to maximize your time aloft (a very common free-flying and contest situation), use as shallow a bank as possible to produce a turn that increases the sink rate as little as possible, yet remains within the confines of the lifting air or the limits of your glide to a safe landing. Remember, any amount of turning increases the glider's sink rate over that of straight ahead flight.

Flying in thermals is an entirely different matter. Thermals consist of a small area or bubble of lift usually surrounded by widespread areas of sink. Thus, in order to maintain altitude or climb in thermal lift, it is necessary to stay within the boundaries of the thermal which of course, requires turning. Furthermore, thermals tend to have uneven lift distributed within the general rising mass. We call these stronger portions "cores" since they are usually near the center of the thermal. It is desireable to remain as near the core as possible, however, once again, too tight a turn (a high bank turn produces a small turn radius) will cause an excessive sink rate. Thus, the best compromise in thermal flying has been found to be a turn of 20 to 30 degrees bank. Only in gentle, consistant thermals would a given bank angle be held continuously. An experienced thermal pilot will vary bank angle to constantly remain in the best lift. Of course, this requires experience and constant monitoring of progress. In stronger thermals, turns as steep as 45° may be required, to remain in the best lift. Small "bullet" thermals occur often in desert areas and these can only be exploited by circling in a steep bank. Generally, the stronger and smaller a thermal is, the steeper the required bank for maximum climb efficiency. These matters are discussed in more detail in Chapter V.

Finally, we have the situation where maneuvers are required in turbalance. this situation is most often seen when landing on a day with strong ground wind or thermals. The object here is to maximize control response and avoid stalls in a turn. The way to proceed in this case is to perform fast turns between 30 and 45 degrees of bank. Flatter turns take longer to produce the required direction change. Also, the stall speed of a flatter turn is a lower percentage of the wind velocity which means an errant gust can produce a stall more readily. Too steep a turn runs the risk of having a turbulent gust bank the wings even steeper resulting in a serious slip close to the ground. Pull on speed before initiating the turn and you will have maximum turn response. Maintain a little extra speed throughout the turn and you will have maximum stall insurance. This extra speed in the turn results in a slip, so monitor your airspeed carefully to maintain safe control. Experiment with these techniques in calm air before you need them in rowdy conditions.

It is apparent that the perfection of turns should be of primary importance to the advancing pilot. There are few flights that don't require efficient, precise turns to work the lift or simply land properly. Practice is the key. Eventually, you will think "turn" and a graceful arc will result. You will look like a hawk wheeling through the sky.

CHAPTER III

THE PERFORMANCE MAP

Besides reminiscing about a sky-out flight, the biggest topic of conversation among hang glider pilots is glider performance. What is glider performance? In actuality, it refers to many things: minimum sink rate, roll rate, slow speed handling, top end, best glide and stability. Some would even go so far as to add weight and ease of set-up as they directly affect the amount of airtime acquired.

In this chapter we will be dealing with minimum sink rate and best glide. These are the matters a pilot has some control over. The other factors that contribute to glider performance are inherent in the design and will be dealt with in later chapters.

A performance map is a plot of a glider's sink rate at varying speeds. This plot will allow us to determine the best speeds to fly in various sink, lift or wind conditions. Just as important, the reader will gain some real insight into how a hang glider performs at various speeds. This will help you choose the right glider for your type of flying.

Another name for a performance map is "polar." We will use polar in the following discussion due to its brevity, although performance map is more descriptive.

PLOTTING THE CURVE

Let's assume you have a sweet little glider that has carried you on many an exciting journey. You may be as comfortable as a cat on a sofa while flying, but still you want to know more about the glider's flying characteristics. How do you go about this investigation?

First you need to obtain a good variometer and airspeed indicator. Then you need to take a few flights on a windless, liftless day. As these conditions are hard to find, the test should be run several times to insure accuracy. Actually, a horizontal wind is permissible, but it's hard to find a wind with no vertical movement when flying from mountains.

The object of the test is to match flying speed with sinking speed at various angles of attack. To do this, you simply hold a certain flying speed on the airspeed indicator and take a reading from your vario. On any given flight, you can probably only remember two or three sets of readings, which is why you should take several flights. The more readings you get, the more accurate your polar will be. Try flying at easy to remember speed (e.g., 15 and 20 mph) and be sure to include your minimum sink speed.

An alternate (and more accurate) method of obtaining airspeed and sink rate readings is to fly at a given bar position over a measured course (say 1000 ft.) while an assistant times you from start to finish with a stop watch. A flagman at the beginning of the course and the timer at the end should have some sort of vertical sighting device so that accurate readings result. The airspeed on a given run will simply be the distance flown (length of course) divided by the time. If feet and seconds are used, this should be converted to miles per hour by multiplying the speed in feet per second by 15/22.

The sink rate through the course can be found by the pilot with an accurate altimeter and a stop watch. The pilot times how long it takes to drop 100 feet at the chosen bar position through the course. The pilot should take several readings at a given bar position for accuracy. Also, flying in both directions through a course and taking the average reading will cancel the effect of wind. With the use of radios, the pilot can call down his readings so that he can run the course several times using different bar positions without having to remember all the data. The sink rate readings will be in feet per second and should be converted to miles per hour by dividing by 88. (There are 60 minutes to an hour and 5,280 feet in a mile, so 60 divided by 5,280 = 1/88.)

As soon as you land, write your data down in the form of lines I and II of Table A, shown in Figure 27. You can use the data in this table to plot a polar directly in a sheet of graph or ruled paper. However, to get it in a form that will allow you to find the glide ratio at different speeds, you should make some conversions.

TABLE A

I	265	250	260	309	340	400	475	V_V IN FPM
II	11	12	14	20	23	27	31	V INDICATED IN MPH
III	18.25	19	20.5	25	27.25	30.4	33.8	V ACTUAL IN MPH
IV	3.01	2.84	2.95	3.52	3.86	4.54	5.40	V_V IN MPH
V	18.0	18.8	20.3	24.7	26.9	30.0	33.4	V_H CALCULATED IN MPH

Figure 27 · Calculating Polar Data

The first thing to note is that the flying speeds indicated by your airspeed meter are not true airspeeds. As mentioned in Chapter I, the air immediately below the wing is pushed along by the glider so that your airspeed indicator reads **slower** than your true airspeed. Figure 28 shows why this is so. To put it simply, a reverse circulation is set up around the wing. If you have an airspeed of 20 mph, for example, the air below the top surface would be traveling about 26 mph. Have you ever noticed that the wind on your face at flying speeds doesn't feel very strong (certainly not as strong as it does when you stick your head out a car window at 20 mph)? This is because your body is in the slower air below the wing.

All airfoils moving through the air cause this reverse flow effect. The pressure below the wing (P1) is greater than the pressure in the free air (P2) which, in turn, is greater than the pressure above the wing (P3). This pressure difference is the cause of lift and drag. The disturbance of the air below the wing diminishes the further you move from the wing. It is insignificant a wingspan or more away. The difference between your actual airspeed and what your indicator reads will depend on how far below your sail it is mounted and your glider's aspect ratio. However, for our purposes, the table in Figure 28 provides accurate enough conversions from indicated to actual airspeed. Using the table in Figure 28, we filled in line III in Table A, Figure 27. We simply wrote the actual airspeed below the indicated airspeed in the table.

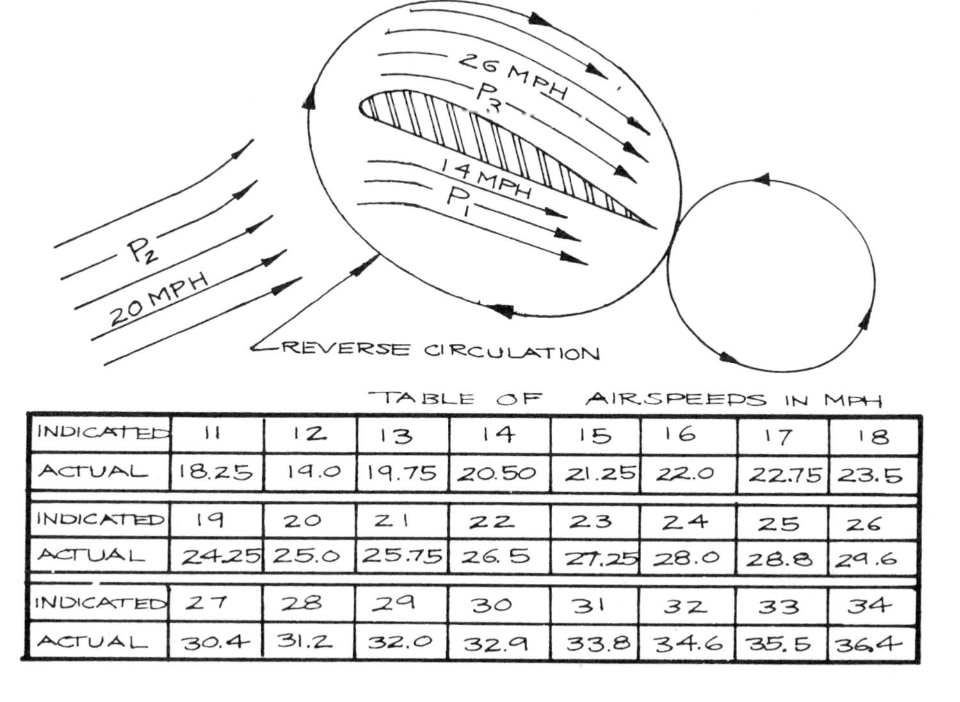

TABLE OF AIRSPEEDS IN MPH

INDICATED	11	12	13	14	15	16	17	18
ACTUAL	18.25	19.0	19.75	20.50	21.25	22.0	22.75	23.5
INDICATED	19	20	21	22	23	24	25	26
ACTUAL	24.25	25.0	25.75	26.5	27.25	28.0	28.8	29.6
INDICATED	27	28	29	30	31	32	33	34
ACTUAL	30.4	31.2	32.0	32.9	33.8	34.6	35.5	36.4

Figure 28 - Indicated and Actual Airspeeds

The next thing we have to do is convert the sink rate and airspeed to the same units. The airspeed indicator gave you the readings in miles per hour (mph), while the variometer gave the readings in feet per minute. So to get both units the same we divide the sink rates by 88. This was done for each sink rate indicated and the results were placed in line IV of Table A.

To understand the final step, take a look at the drawing in Figure 27. Here we see a glider following a glide path described by the arrow (vector) V. The length of this arrow is proportional to the airspeed. We can separate the velocity of the glider (V) into a horizontal component (Vh) and a vertical component (Vv). The horizontal component is the horizontal velocity and the vertical component represents the sink rate.

We saw in Chapter I that the glide ratio is equal to Vh / Vv. However, what we have in our data Table A is V (flying velocity) and Vv (sink rate). Consequently, we must convert V to Vh. This is easy once we see we have a right triangle and use the basic rule: the square of the hypotenuse of a right triangle is equal to the sum of the squares of the remaining two sides. Manipulating this to our purposes, we have $Vh = \sqrt{V^2 - Vv^2}$. Since we know V and Vv at several points, we can find Vh at these points also.

The results of the above calculations are included in line V of Table A. A sample calculation made from the first data point is $Vh = \sqrt{18.25^2 - 3.01^2} =$ 18.00 mph.

Now we can plot a curve on graph paper using Vv as the vertical axis, and Vh as the horizontal axis. The results using the data from Table A is shown in Figure 29. Note that the units for Vv are given in both miles per hour and feet per minute for clarity.

To summarize the method of plotting your glider's polar, put the data you found in flight in a table. Now convert the indicated airspeed to actual airspeed using the table in Figure 28. Next, convert the sink rates in feet per minute to miles per hour by dividing by 88. Finally, find Vh from V and Vv by using the formula. Plot this data and you have a nicely shaped polar curve.

At this point, you may be saying, "Why should I spend time hassling with math and graphs when I could be out soaring a ridge." The real reason is that the information you are about to discover will help you soar that ridge and fly cross-country. In addition, the introduction of test vehicles allows the designer himself to construct a polar plot of a glider. Hopefully, it will become an industry standard policy to supply a polar plot with every glider they sell. Sailplane manufacturers often follow this policy. Thus, you will be saved the job of testing and calculating, but you should know how to interpret a polar. Hang gliding is becoming more sophisticated and an advanced pilot should constantly work to increase his understanding.

Now let's interpret our graph. Note that we have plotted our seven data points by first finding the horizontal velocity on the Vh axis then dropping straight down until we come to the sink rate that matches it. For the first point in our table we drop down from the horizontal velocity of 18 mph until we reach a sink rate of 3.01 mph or 265 fpm.

Since we are dealing with variable conditions, your points may not match up to define a smooth curve. In that case, draw a curve that most nearly touches all the points. You should discard any point that is too far out of line. Once again, the advantage of performing multiple tests is a greater number of plotted points to insure accuracy. Possible sources of error are your airspeed indicator and the presence of vertically moving air. Be sure to perform these tests out of ground effect and well away from the hill in still air to minimize the latter source of error. As long as you are consistent with the use of your airspeed indicator, and convert your observed speed to actual airspeed, you will have valid data. You can compare polars from two different gliders by using the same set of instruments on each glider. Any error in the instruments will be equal for both gliders.

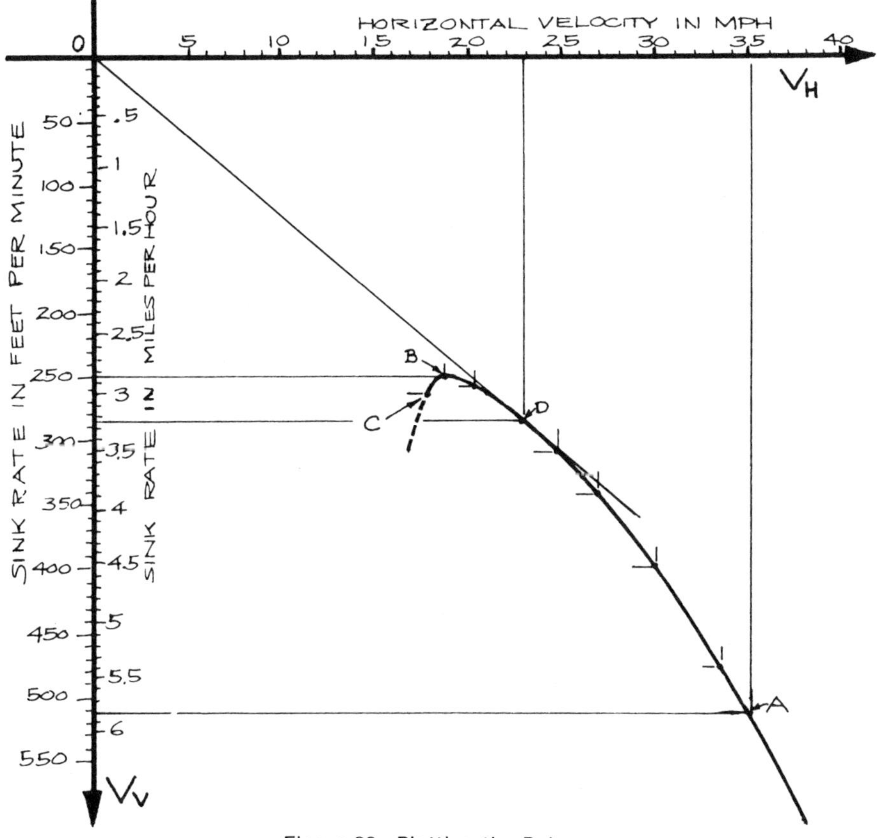

Figure 29 · Plotting the Polar

Immediately, you should see that you can read your sink rate for any speed. Choose a speed on the horizontal axis (for example – 35 mph) then drop down to the curve. You arrive at point A. Now move across to the vertical axis and you read the sink rate as 510 fpm. Note that we used the horizontal velocity Vh, not the actual flying speed of the glider V. However, V is only about a half mile per hour faster than Vh at this point, so the error is insignificant.

The minimum sink rate is the highest point the curve reaches. This is at B, one of the data points. Part of the glider starts to stall at B, so the lift is reduced and the sink rate increases. This continues to some point C where a full break stall develops. The portion of the curve from B to C consists of parachuting flight.

What about glide ratio? The polar doesn't fail us here either. We can find the glide ratio at any flying speed. Simply choose any point on the plotted curve, find the Vh and Vv values at this point then divide Vh by Vv (use mph for Vv). The glide ratio is always equal to the horizontal velocity divided by the vertical velocity. In this manner, the glide ratio of your glider can be found at any flying speed.

The glide ratio that interests us most is the maximum glide ratio. You can find this as shown in Figure 30. Simply take a straight edge and draw a tangent to the curve from the point of intersection of the axis. This is line OA in the figure. Why is this the maximum glide ratio? Because it gives you the highest value of the fraction Vh / Vv. To see for yourself, choose points on the curve on either side of point A such as B and C. When you calculate the glide ratios, you will find they are less than at A. (The fraction Vh / Vv is actually the inverse of the slope of any line drawn from the origin. Thus, the line that has the least slope will represent the greatest glide ratio. This is always the tangent OA.)

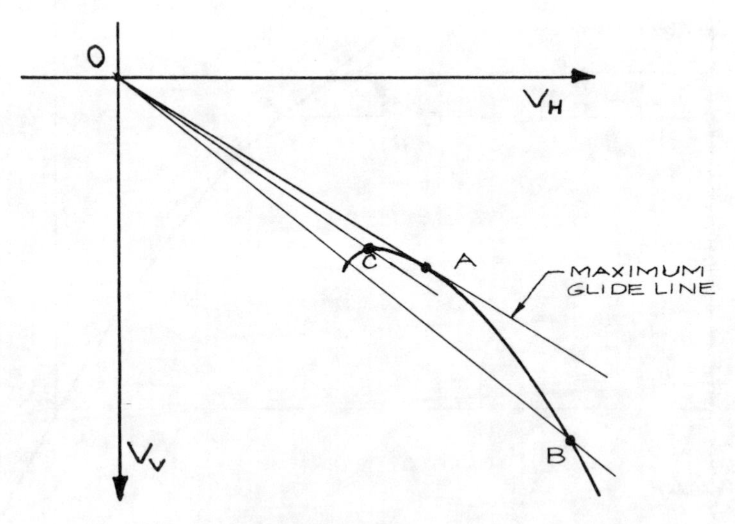

Figure 30 · Finding Maximum Glide

Now go back to Figure 29 and find the maximum glide ratio of our hypothetical glider. Take a straight edge and position it at O then swing it down until it hits the curve. This will be the point of best glide. This point is labeled D. The horizontal velocity at D is 22.8 mph while the vertical velocity is 3.28 mph. The calculated maximum glide ratio is then about 7 to 1. This will occur at a flying speed of about 23 mph. Now we have another way of finding our glider's "best glide speed" (see Chapter I).

It is interesting to note that at the minimum sink rate point, the glide ratio is worse than at the maximum glide point; conversely, the sink rate at best glide is greater than at the minimum sink point. There are many other things we can learn from a polar. We will divide these into two subjects: speed to fly and performance factors.

SPEED TO FLY

In Chapter I we demonstrated that flying your "best glide speed" in the air doesn't necessarily get you anywhere over the ground. For example, the glider in Figure 29 could be flying at 23 mph to get the best glide ratio, but in a 25 mph wind would actually be moving backwards 2 mph. This doesn't exactly put forth a good showing when it comes to reaching a landing area upwind. Obviously, if the pilot sped up he would make some headway, although his sink rate would increase. How much should he speed up? By using the polar of the glider we can find the exact speed to fly to maximize our distance over the ground in any wind condition.

It is assumed that the pilot wants to go as far as he can. If he wanted to stay up as long as possible, he would simply fly at minimum sink speed or as slow as he could. Let's imagine the pilot is flying in a 10 mph headwind. By now you should know that he should speed up somewhat.

Look at Figure 31. Starting at the origin, move to the right to point A at

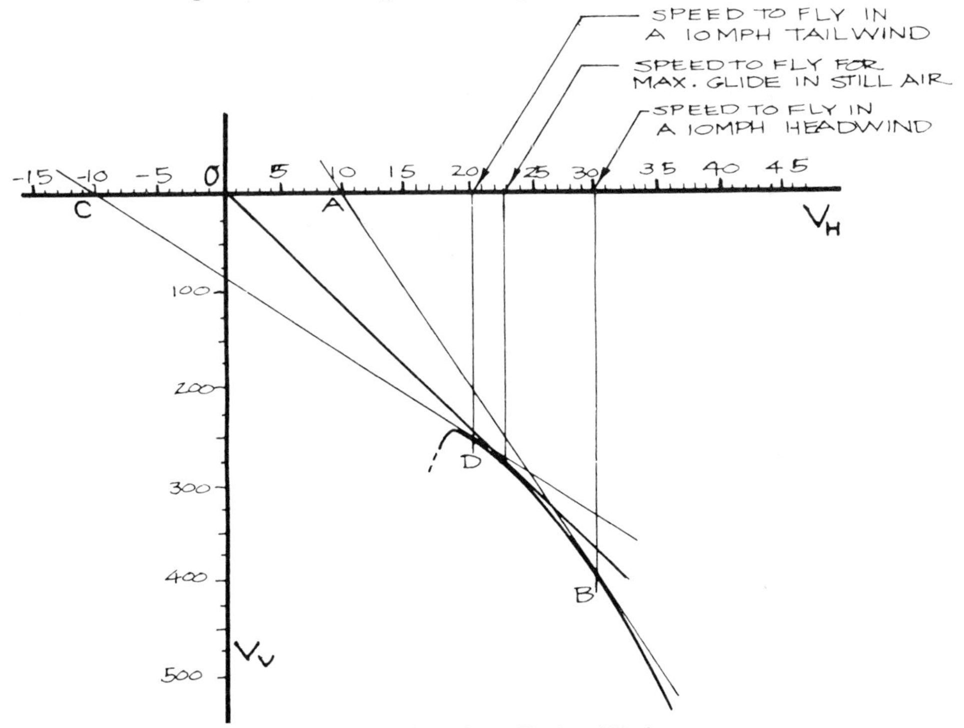

Figure 31 · Speeds to Fly in a Wind

10 mph. This is where the origin is displaced due to the headwind. Using point A as a pivot, we can now draw a tangent to the curve AB. The speed to fly for best distance over the gound in a 10 mph headwind is then given by point B. This requires a flying speed of about 30 mph. Note the sink rate has increased to 400 mph, but the pilot still covers the most ground.

A tailwind is equally easy to handle. For a 10 mph tailwind, you move to the left 10 mph on the Vh axis and draw the tangent from this point to the polar curve (line CD). The speed to fly to achieve point D is about 20 mph with a sink rate of 260 fpm. From this we can conclude that a headwind gives you a poorer glide ratio over the ground while a tailwind improves the glide.

What about lift and sink? You may know that you want to speed up in sink and slow up in lift. How much? This is shown in Figure 32. If you are in 100 fpm sink, for example, move up the vertical axis to point A. The tangent from A to B tells you how fast to fly.

If you are in 100 fpm lift, move down to point C and again draw the tangent. Point D will give you the speed to fly. It should be apparent that if the lift is greater than your minimum sink rate you don't fly slower than your minimum sink speed – you would be stalled!

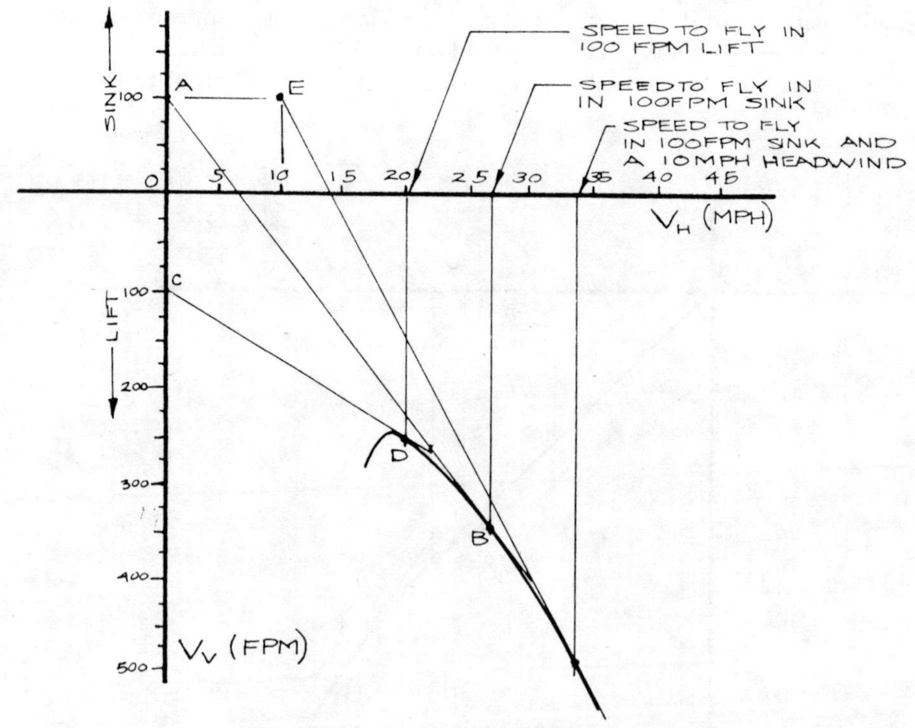

Figure 32 · Speed to Fly in Sink or Lift

Now consider a combination of vertical and horizontal air movement. All you have to do is move along the horizontal axis the proper amount and direction then move along the vertical axis the proper amount and direction and place a point. For example, if you are flying in a 10 mph headwind with 100 fpm sink, you would arrive at point E and draw a tangent from here. In a crosswind, you must determine the component of the wind that hits you either as a headwind or a tailwind. You then apply this to your polar curve to figure out the speed to fly.

Obviously, you can't memorize all the speeds to fly for different conditions. In addition, you may read a given sink rate on your variometer, but how do you know whether the air is sinking or your glider is diving. Actually, you can't unless you also have an airspeed indicator. However, you can fly at your "best glide speed," note the sink rate on your variometer and speed up or slow down according to whether you detect sink or lift. How much you change speed depends on how strong the sink and lift are.

For a headwind or tailwind, there isn't much you learn from your instruments. However, the method for finding your best glide explained in Chapter I will prove valuable here. That is, a point in front of you will move down if your glide will take you beyond it. A point will move up if you are on a glide path that will fall short of the point. This method will work in lift, sink, or horizontal wind. You simply vary your speed until you get the maximum glide over the ground.

The real value of the polar graph is teaching you how your glider performs in different conditions. By looking at the actual values of glide and sink, you can get a better idea of how to fly these conditions. Note that you speed up a lot more above "best glide speed" in a 10 mph headwind than you slow down for a 10 mph tailwind. Similarly, flying efficiently in sink requires you to speed up much more than you slow up in lift.

PERFORMANCE FACTORS

There are several matters concerning glider performance that can be illuminated by looking at a polar. The first of these is wing loading. What happens to your performance when you add or subtract weight from your glider? If you increase weight, you know you increase flying speeds but keep the same maximum glide ratio. Let's picture this. Figure 33 shows the polars of a glider flown at two different wing loadings. Curve AA is with a 150 pound pilot and curve BB is with a 190 pound pilot. The curve simply moves down the best glide tangent OC when you add weight. The light pilot achieves his minimum sink rate at 18 mph, while the heavier pilot achieves his at a little under 20 mph (remember, you speed up 0.5 mph for every 10 lbs additional weight).

Both pilots achieve the same maximum glide ratio. The lighter pilot has the best sink rate. Now look what happens in a headwind. Assume a 10 mph headwind and move to the 10 mph point on the right side of the Vh axis. This is point D. Now if we draw tangents to the curves AA and BB, we see that the pilot with the heaviest wing loading has the best glide over the ground. This is not to say the heaviest pilot has the best sink rate, but he will go further upwind than his lighter buddy, provided he flies the right speed.

Now imagine the air is sinking 100 fpm. Move up the Vv axis and mark the point. The tangent drawn from this point to the curves will again indicate that the heavier pilot has a better glide capability. However, if the pilots encounter a tailwind or lift, the lighter pilot has the glide ratio advantage. Try this on the graph. A general rule we can form is: in lift or a tailwind, lighter wing loadings are better; in sink or a headwind, heavier wing loadings are better. This will have significance when we discuss thermals in Chapter V.

In certain wind conditions a heavier pilot even has a better sink rate than a lighter pilot on the same glider. This is when the wind is strong. The two curves in Figure 33 intersect at point E. This is at an airspeed of 23 mph. If the gliders were flying at an airspeed greater than 23 mph to penetrate a wind or in in a speed run, the pilot of a heavier glider would find that his performance is superior in both sink rate and glide ratio. This is a phenomena that all pilots should be aware of when competing or soaring on strong days. Light wing loadings are great for maxing out light lift days, but performance really falls off when higher speeds are required.

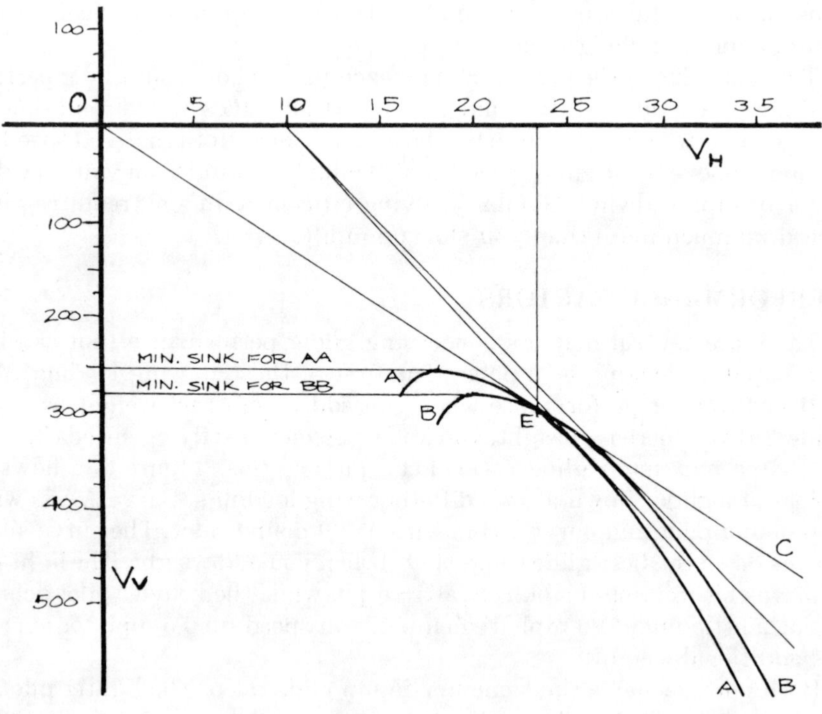

Figure 33 · Wing Loading Effects

What makes the polar curve drop off at higher speeds? Parasitic drag, of all sorts. The cables, control bar, king post, assundry hardware, harness and most of all, the pilot interrupts the airflow and creates drag. Parasitic drag increases as the square of the velocity. If we increase the speed a little bit, the drag increases a lot. Consequently, performance falls off as we speed up.

Figure 34 compares the polar of a high performance hang glider with a sailplane. Note how the low drag (streamlined) body of the sailplane prevents the polar from falling off at higher speeds. The glide ratio and sink rate are better for the sailplane and the flying speeds are greater.

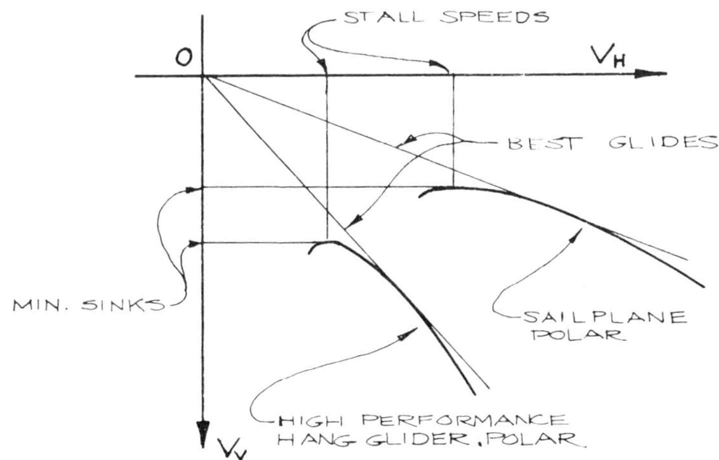

Figure 34 · Comparison of Polars

Besides having lower drag, a sailplane also has a higher aspect ratio. How does this affect the polar and hence performance? Aspect ratio is a measure of the "thinness" of a wing when viewed from above. Higher aspect ratio wings reduce the amount of induced drag created. However, since induced drag is only present at slow speeds, higher aspect ratios (long slim wings) do nothing for performance at high speeds. In fact, due to the added parasitic drag that higher aspect ratios require (longer cross bars, leading edges, etc.), there is a limit to the usefulness of increasing aspect ratio in a hang glider.

Figure 35 shows two gliders of the same general construction but with varying aspect ratios. Curve BB has the higher aspect ratio. Note how both

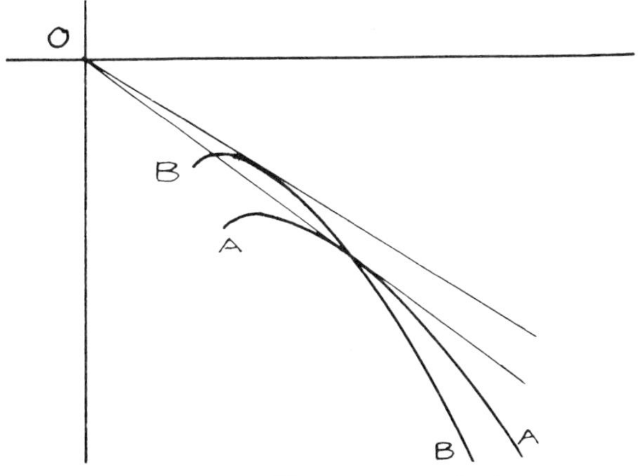

Figure 35 · Effect of Aspect Ratio

the sink rate and glide ratio are improved. Also, the flying speeds are slowed somewhat. The higher aspect ratio glider does suffer a bit more loss of performance at higher speeds. Usually a higher aspect ratio glider is flown at slightly higher wing loadings to bring the flying up a bit, but the high speed loss is still there.

There are many more concepts that can be learned from analyzing the polar curve of a glider. However, most of these matters are for designers to mull over in their endless search for the ultimate performing wing. We pilots must be content with getting the most performance possible out of our present glider. We can best accomplish this by familiarizing ourselves with our own glider's polar.

CHAPTER IV

THE ART OF FLYING

Although this book and others like it endeavor to apply scientific principles to explain flying technique, the fact remains that flying is an art. We can reduce the basic maneuvers to exact quantities, but we can only suggest methods, policies and plans when it comes to an actual flight in varying conditions. The pilot is always relying on his judgment and general skill to fly safely and efficiently.

In this chapter we will look at proven methods of handling different situations as well as improving a pilot's judgment. The real determinant in the development of good judgment is attitude. A good pilot will never be an expert pilot if he doesn't have the proper mental attitude. An expert pilot sees his limits with a wide margin for error. He only "goes for it" when he knows he can make it. With a great accumulation of airtime, he is not so eager to rush off the mountain into a gale. He knows the wind will always blow and the mountain will not move. He bides his time.

The whole question boils down to one thing: maturity. If a pilot is mature, he will fly safely. If he flies safely, his confidence and skill will build steadily. He will relax in the air so that his judgment is unimpaired. His flight decisions will be flawless.

INSTRUMENTS

In every pilot's quest to fly further and higher, there comes a time when he asks himself if instruments will help him attain his goal. He reasons that more knowledge of the conditions and his present performance will aid his decision making. This is true on the condition that the pilot doesn't rely solely on the instruments.

If you learned to fly hang gliders using instruments from the start, chances are you may be overly dependent on these electro-mechanical devices. The problem is, you may never develop an automatic feel for airspeed or an automatic sense of control. Try flying without your instruments. If you feel uncomfortable and lost, perhaps you should spend some time learning to judge airspeed, work the lift and set up landings using your own senses. When your return to using your instruments, you should rely on them only to help you map the sky's lift patterns and fly at the best speed through this lift.

The most important instrument you can purchase is a variometer. A vario (short for variometer) is a device that indicates vertical motion. When you move up or down in flight, your vario lets you know how fast this motion is through a visual readout, an audio signal or both. Visual readouts are usually in the form of a dial or a pellet moving along a scale, while audio signals can be anything from a soft wailing or hum to the chirping of a robin in heat. Most varios alter the audio tone as vertical motion changes. Some produce an audio signal during upward motion or lift conditions only.

By what mysterious method do these little black boxes detect a change in vertical velocity? All the vario designs currently used for hang gliding simply measure the changing air pressure as a pilot climbs or descends. As you know, the higher you go, the lower the pressure of the air (a drop of about 3% per thousand feet normally occurs). We can create an altimeter (to indicate how high we are) simply by measuring the absolute pressure at any level, while a variometer measures the rate of change of this pressure. The greater our vertical velocity, the greater the rate of change of pressure we will detect.

There are three basic vario designs on the market. These are shown schematically in Figure 36. The first drawing shows a typical pellet variometer. In this design, a flask, insulated to reduce temperature effects, is connected to two tapered chambers containing a pellet in each. As the variometer rises, pressure drops which results in the flow of air out of the flask. This air flows through the chambers and raises one pellet. The greater the change in pressure, the faster the flow and thus, the higher the pellet rises. When the motion is downward, air flows into the flask raising the pellet in the other chamber.

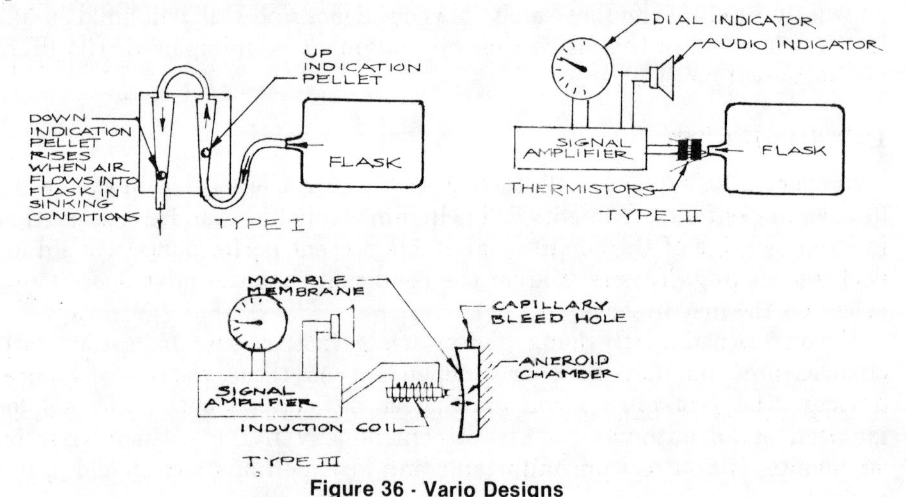

Figure 36 · Vario Designs

The second vario design uses a similar flask arrangement, while the in and out air flow is detected by electronic means. Flow sensors (consisting of heat sensitive resistors, or thermistors) produce a signal which is amplified, then tailored to drive the visual and audio output.

The third drawing illustrates the varios that dispense with the flask and use a small enclosed chamber or aneroid to detect pressure changes. Instead of sensing air flow, a movable membrane varies the core position of a coil (inductor) as pressure changes force the membrane in or out. A small bleed hole or capillary is opened in the aneroid chamber to allow air to enter and escape in a limited manner. Thus, if you stop vertical movement, the pressure inside the aneroid chamber equalizes with the pressure outside, reducing the output signal to zero. On the other hand, if vertical motion continues, the pressure inside the chamber will not match the outside pressure and an output signal will result. The size of the capillary hole determines the sensitivity of this type of instrument.

A fourth vario design (not pictured) incorporates a pressure transducer – a small electronic device designed specifically to measure fluid pressure. A signal from the transducer is used to produce the output variations. These designs are becoming common as they make the smallest packages.

If you expect your vario to last for years, you must take good care of it. Avoid hard knocks, bumps and vibrations. Hard landings are as bad for your vario as they are for your glider (if you haven't perfected your landings, you should not consider using a vario – first things first).

The best way to mount your vario is on an arm that detaches from the glider or directly to the control bar with hose clamps. When you are done flying, remove your vario and cradle it in your helmet or harness for stowing in your flight bag.

The next most useful instrument for monitoring your flight is an altimeter. This device lets you know how high you are above a prescribed level. An altimeter measures the absolute pressure drop as you gain altitude (not the rate of change of pressure like a variometer). You can set your altimeter to zero either at the landing area, take-off point or some other elevation and thus have a reading at all times of how high you are above the point you chose. When flying in areas of regular aircraft use, set your altimeter to sea level (find out the elevation above sea level of your take-off point from a topographic map) so that you will know where to look for airplanes at various altitudes. Remember, when flying without instruments, airplanes are supposed to be at even thousands plus 500 feet when heading westerly (from 180 to 359 degrees). Similarly, airplanes should fly at odd thousands plus 500 feet when heading easterly (0 to 179 degrees). In general, the more expensive your altimeter is, the more accurate and compact it is (weight is still our biggest enemy). However, the needs of hang gliding do not require too much accuracy or sensitivity in an altimeter (20 foot increments is plenty) as long as the reading increases when you rise and decreases when you drop.

The information you receive from your altimeter is important for safety and peformance reasons. Knowing your altitude above a ridge is a prerequisite for following the lift over the top. You should also make constant use of an altimeter if you are flying at high altitudes. Remember, 12,500 ft. is the limit for flying without oxygen.

One of the best uses of an altimeter is for providing a progress report.

After some minutes of working lift and avoiding sink, only your altimeter will tell you if you have actually achieved any net gain of altitude. When used in conjunction with a variometer, an altimeter helps you maximize your time in the upward air.

Airspeed indicators are common flight companions, but are often overused. A hang glider pilot is riding free in the airstream, and consequently can use his senses to detect airspeed. Airspeed indicators mounted on the conrol bar do not read true airspeed. The indicated velocity immediately below the glider will be 5 or more mph slower than the actual speed the glider is moving through the air (this matter is discussed in Chapter III). Thus, an airspeed indicator can only provide relative (not actual) airspeed information. This is fine, but a pilot can learn to judge airspeed just as readily by feeling and hearing the air rush by him, as well as using the control bar position as an auxilary angle-of-attack check. If you must use an airspeed indicator, you must not rely on it to let you know when you are near stall. Stall recovery often requires a quick reaction and the time required to check your airspeed indicator will make matters worse. You can feel a stall by noting the sluggishness of the glider to small roll inputs and the lack of wind in your face.

There are those pilots that eschew instruments entirely in their quest for bird-like freedom. This is an admirable attitude but much practice is required to develop the ability to out-think a variometer. The body can only sense an acceleration. This means that when you fly into a puff of lift, you may feel the initial jolt, but once you settle down to an even climb rate, you will have no feeling of being lifted. This is also true in sink. Watching another glider can be deceiving, for you both may be in sink, but he may be in greater sink. It would then appear that you are rising compared to him. If you interpreted this to indiate that you were in lift, you would be greatly mistaken.

Since the body can't feel the difference between a steady 500 feet per minute down and 500 feet per minute up, how do we get rid of the vario? The technique requires the use of your eyes. Near the ridge or mountain top, you can watch the terrain below you and at the horizon. When you're moving up, the terrain will appear to recede and the horizon will move down in your field of vision. As you get higher (above 1000 feet or so), you can make use of the fact that as you move away from a group of objects, they will appear to come together. As you approach this group, the objects will appear to separate. This is illustrated in Figure 37.

Objects on the ground such as trees, buildings, boulders or other irregularities will seem to pull together as you rise and move apart as you drop. You must watch carefully directly below you to detect his apparent motion. Below 1000 ft. your forward motion confuses this latter technique. In addition, the higher you are above the ground, the less sensitive this method is, since the smaller the apparent change is for a given upward velocity. Certainly much practice is required to replace a vario with an "eyeball" method. The subtle speed variations necessary for cross-country flying may never be achieved without a vario. However, it is still exciting to explore the limits of man's ability to experience flight as unfettered as the soaring birds.

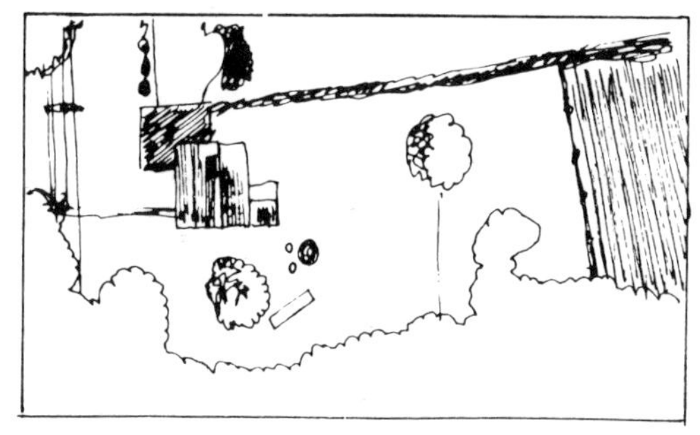

Figure 37 - Judging Vertical Velocity

FLYING AT ALTITUDE

One of the processes that a pilot experiences is a gradual increase in the feeling of security at higher and higher altitudes. A beginner's tentative ground skimming forays are often terrifying, but soon he is flying over the treetops with relaxed ease. Likewise, a pilot's first sudden flight with a thousand feet of ground clearance is often tinged with fright and tainted by the "dive syndrome." However, learning to relax at higher altitudes is not too hard, especially if the pilot is well prepared with knowledge of the unseen conditions.

What are the dangers of flying at higher altitudes? Surprisingly, for the most part, there are fewer dangers than there are when flying near the ground. At low altitudes, a pilot must contend with shifting air currents and turbulence caused by ground obstructions. He must always be aware of his position in relation to his landing field, the ridge top, areas of sink, wind shadow, power lines, trees and other potential hazards. At higher altitudes he must only worry about turbulence associated with shear lines and thermals.

Thermals grow in size and tend to slow in rate of ascent as they climb higher. They lose bouyancy through mixing with the surrounding air. Consequently, the turbulence associated with thermals tends to be lessened at greater heights. Exceptions to this are during superadiabatic lapse rate (SALR) conditions and when the wind gets dramatically stronger at altitudes. A SALR occurs most often over the desert and tends to accelerate thermals even at high altitudes, due to the great temperature difference between the air at the ground and aloft. Thus, the turbulence created as the thermal bubbles upward through the ambient air remains strong at thousands of feet above the ground. Indeed, mid-day desert conditions are often unflyable at any altitude due to the many small bone-jarring thermals.

When the wind is strong at higher altitudes, thermals will be torn apart as they rise into the faster moving airstream. This, of course, causes turbulence. However, since the action of thermals tends to speed up the surface winds (by mixing the air at various levels) to the velocity of the upper winds, the air will exhibit similar turbulence at all levels. Thus, we can conclude that if we can fly safely near the ground in thermal conditions then we will be safe at any altitude. Of course, we must avoid the underside of dark, building cumulus clouds (see Thermal Flying) as these formidable giants like to gobble gliders. Shear lines occur when two different masses of air rub each other the wrong way. For instance, shear can occur when a cool seabreeze front conflicts with the warm land air. Winds converging from different sides of a mountain can meet at the top and cause a shear line. Warm air moving over colder air nestled in a valley can also cause shear. Of course, the movement of a classic cold or warm front is always accompanied with shear line turbulence.

How do you avoid such turbulence? Shear lines in general are hard to predict, however, for the altitude flyer we can adopt a few safe practices. First, be aware of the conditions at all levels as you progress up a mountain to take-off. Wind moving in markedly different directions at take-off and in the landing area should indicate that somewhere a shifting occurs that may be accompanied by shear turbulence. Also, warmer temperatures at the take-off than in the landing area indicates a warm layer moving over the lower cold layer. (The air is normally cooler as you move higher. If it is not, an inversion exists.) Shear turbulence can exist between the moving layers. In general be wary of any unusual wind direction or velocity changes as well as radical temperature changes at different levels.

Be righteously fearful of flying in the vicinity of fronts. Large cold or warm fronts announce their presence with dark clouds and rain. It's pretty easy to avoid these frontal conditions. Smaller seabreeze fronts can move rapidly and are sometimes more insidious. Their outline can often be discerned by the difference in visibility on either side of the front due to the different moisture content. Debris, dust, clouds and soaring birds may also be floating in the lifting air at the front. When soaring in coastline conditions, be wary of the sudden return of the land breeze and shear turbulence, especially when the circulating action is reduced as the sun sinks in the late afternoon (see Figure 38).

During thermal conditions, shear lines tend to be attenuated or dampened out, since thermals punch into the inversion layer and even out the wind through mixing. Thus, we can make the following generalizations about the safety of flying high altitudes: in thermal conditions you will be safe as long as you carefully judge the strength of the thermals and avoid over-powering boomers at take-off. If the air is stable, chances are you achieve altitude by flying from a high point to a lower landing area. This allows you to check for possible shear conditions at different levels as you drive up to launch. It should be noted that much caution is required when flying with an engine on a hang glider since a pilot can power up to an area of shear without the capability of being warned ahead of time. With a conservative plan for avoiding high altitude turbulence, and a bit of time spent floating a few thousand feet above the ground, you will soon be planning cross country sightseeing flights.

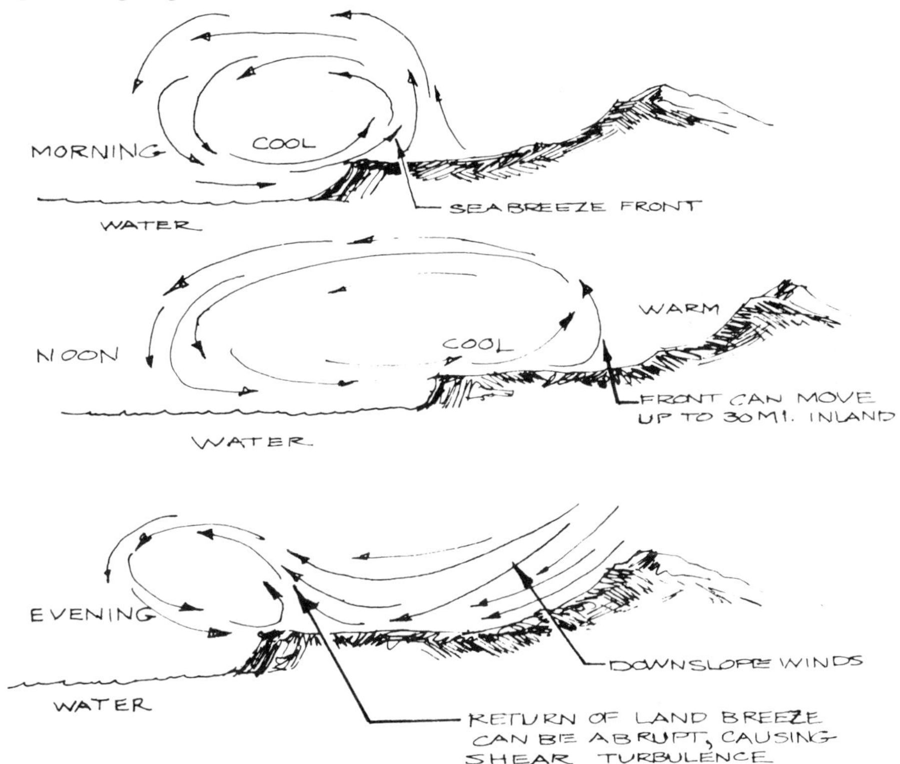

Figure 38 · Seabreeze Cycles

It should be obvious that by the time you are flying with thousands of feet of ground clearance you should be judging airspeed flawlessly. Above a thousand feet, the ground seems to barely move; there's only you and the wind. Since the air gets thinner as you climb higher, you may wonder how this affects your airspeed. Actually, all speeds (stall speed, minimum sink, best glide, etc.) are increased 1.5 percent for every 1,000 ft. gain in altitude. However, you cannot recognize this while flying. Due to the thinner air you will feel the same pressure on your face at stall speed at a high elevation as a low elevation. Your glider experiences the same thing. It moves faster to develop the same amount of lift and drag it did at lower elevations. Your maximum glide ratio remains the same while your sink rate increases 1.5 percent per 1,000 ft. Your vario reads the same minimum sink at all altitudes since it too is fooled by the thinner air.

Although you can't notice the effects of altitude while flying, you can (and must) be aware of differences when taking off from elevated points. Your take-off speed will be increased in the same manner as your flying speed. Thus, if you have to run 17 mph to get airborne at sea level, you'll have to run 19.55 mph at 10,000 ft. This could lead to skinned knees for the slow or unprepared pilot.

FLYING IN TURBULENCE

If the air did not move, we would experience no turbulence. Of course, there would be no thermals, ridge lift or waves to keep us aloft for hours. To know the joys of soaring, we must contend with a certain amount of turbulence.

Every pilot that has been flying for some time has encountered turbulence. The cause of turbulence can be divided into three categories: ground obstructions and terrain irregularities disrupting the airflow, thermals pushing upward and shear between two air masses (for more detail see *Flying Conditions* by the author). In general, turbulence is the random swirling of the air. A pilot encountering these swirls or eddies will feel light bumps (textured air) or heavy duty jerks (rodeo air), depending on the energy of the swirls.

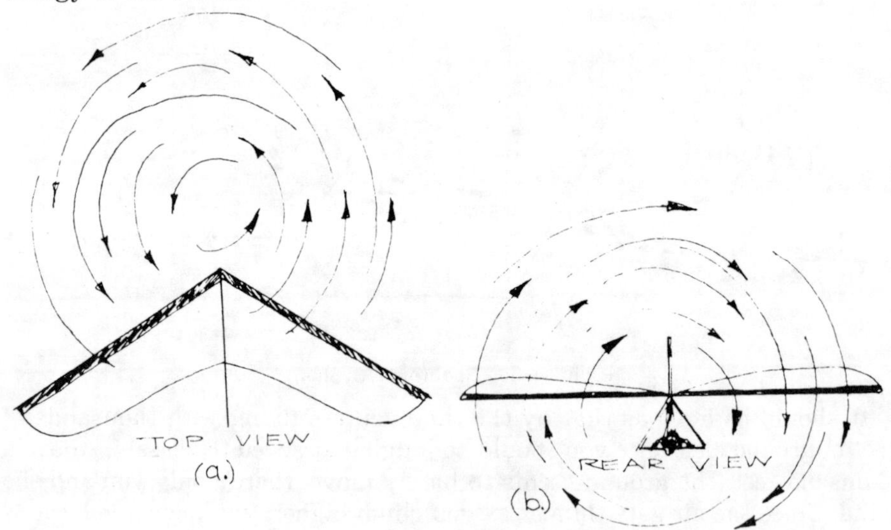

Figure 39 · Turbulent Eddies

Before we investigate the best flying technique in turbulence, let's look at how it affects our gliders. Assume that a glider encounters a turbulent eddy with a vertical axis of rotation as in Figure 39(a). Here we see the left wing will feel an increase in the relative wind while the right wing will feel as if its airspeed was suddenly reduced. The left wing will then lift up and back while the right wing will accelerate down and forward. Thus we can imagine the glider rolling to the right and yawing to the left.

In a similar manner, a glider flying into a turbulent eddy with a longitudinal axis of rotation as in Figure 39(b) would experience a lifting and forward movement with the left wing, while the right wing drops down and back. Here the glider rolls right and yaws right.

Both of these types of eddies cause the glider to yaw and roll. The first situation simulates an adverse yaw condition while the second situation is identical to a coordinated right turn. The correction for both cases calls for a quick move to the left of the bar to roll the glider level. If the eddies were rotating in the opposite direction, the pilot would have to move to the right side to straighten the glider out. The main idea is to react against the roll inputs you feel from the turbulence with quick, accurate movements. You cannot expect to stop the glider from yawing by swinging your body; let the glider's yaw-roll coupling take care of yawing while you make roll corrections.

A third eddy orientation is shown in Figure 40(a). Here the glider flies into air moving downward, then air moving upward as it passes through the swirl. A pilot encountering this situation would feel his nose lifted then a sharp dive as his nose is dropped and his tail lifted. This feeling is often encountered when flying downwind in turbulence near the ground since the turbulence tends to "roll" with the orientation shown.

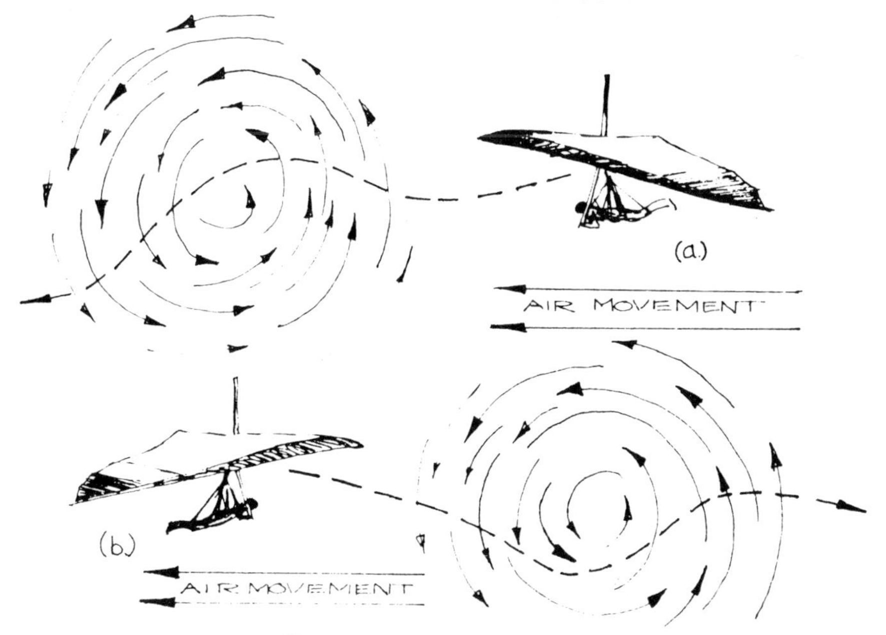

Figure 40 · Turbulent Eddies

When a pilot enters a similar eddy moving upwind he feels his nose drop then a sudden rearing of his glider as in 40(b). The control movements to make in both these cases is pitch corrections opposing the disturbance made by the turbulence. If the turbulence is strong, be cautious of over-correcting. You may push out to combat a turbulence-induced dive, only to be hit with an up-draft that immediately stalls you. In this situation you should make the necessary roll corrections, but keep pitch corrections to a minimum. Hold the control bar slightly in from best glide position and let the stability of the glider take care of the rest. Obviously, if you are pitched radically nose-up or into a vertical dive you should react suddenly and stongly, but quick, bobbing pitch changes are best handled by riding them like a boat on a choppy bay.

Keep your speed moderate and your bank angles reduced in turbulence. This is especially true in thermal conditions. A low angle of attack (high flying speed) or a steep bank angle can be made worse by the right turbulent gust. In addition, the slower you fly the lower the stresses on the glider (and your body) as a swirl slams it around. Maintain just enough speed to maneuver properly. This will be about your best glide speed. As you approach the ground for landing gradually slow up. By the time you are within ten feet of the ground you should be moving fairly slowly. There is a possibility that you may be stalled in this situation, but it is better to risk a stall and a slightly hard landing than to be slammed to the ground while moving 20 mph.

The turbulence in thermals represents a special case. Often a glider is dumped "over-the-falls" when flying through a thermal. This is a common occurrence in small, powerful thermals. The center of the thermal consists of a strong updraft while the outside billows out and down. A glider exiting the thermal may have lift on its tail while its nose is in a downdraft. The result: a sudden heart-in-the-mouth dive. An experienced pilot can cope with this condition by being alert and prepared. He should expect this type of treatment from any thermal he enters and he should be ready to counter by putting the control bar at a moderate speed position. Obviously, not every thermal is going to tip you on your nose. After you have been in the air awhile you will have a general idea of the nature of the thermal turbulence and you can relax your guard if the lift proves to be non-vicious.

Another effect of thermals is to lift one wing and turn you against your wishes. All your grumbling and struggling seems to do no good in this case. Generally, you should continue to fight against the thermal since the lift is usually in the area you are being forced away from. Try pulling in the bar to gain a little speed to help you out-wrestle the thermal. The most important thing is to persevere until you are once again the master and turning in the direction you want to go.

A final source of turbulence frequently encountered in hang gliding is wing tip vortices. These organized swirls created by all flying craft can be hazardous since they consist of a lot of air moving in the same manner. Vortices tend to move together and downward as they expand after leaving the wingtips (see Figure 41). You can learn to avoid the wake turbulence of other gliders by not passing too close behind them. While soaring a ridge, you will probably miss the vortices from a glider passing in front of you at your altitude since the upward moving air will carry them above you. If you are too close behind another glider however, be prepared for some hard sudden chops. Hold on and make corrections as you would for any type of turbulence.

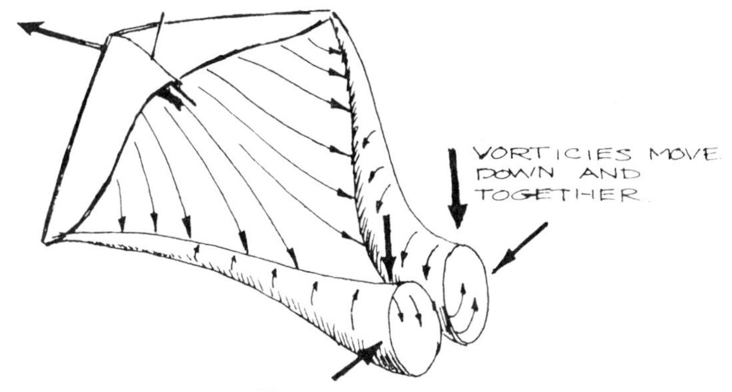

Figure 41 · Tip Vortices

Vortices from airplanes and helicopters are a real danger. Uninformed pilots of these craft let curiosity get the better of their judgment and sometimes cruise in for a close-up look at hang gliding. If these pilots were aware of how their aircraft functioned (as they should be) they wouldn't think of such an act. However, there are plenty of unaware pilots, so you must be ready to take evasive action. Make no mistake – vortices from even small airplanes can knock you out of the sky. Helicopters are even worse (they produce the strongest turbulence when they are hovering). Waving an airplane away may be mistaken for a friendly greeting. The best course of action when confronted with an approaching aircraft is to fly away from it and get to the ground as quickly as possible. Vortices from large aircraft can linger for many minutes and will drift with the wind. If an aircraft is passing near, the air is no place for you. The best policy for preventing such problems is to request the airports around your flying sites to inform the local pilots of your activity and their threat to your safety. Of course, you must be aware of, and stay clear of controlled airspace.

FLYING IN RIDGE LIFT

The first attempts at ridge soaring comes early in a pilot's career. Modern gliders allow an inexperienced pilot to learn to soar in light winds. By the time he has reached the advanced level he hs logged many hours on the ridge, in all types of conditions. He should not conclude, however, that he knows all there is to learn about ridge soaring. (For a complete discussion on learning to soar, see page 82 in the book *Hang Gliding Flying Skills* by Dennis Pagen.)

There are many different types, shapes and sizes of ridges so any guidelines for flying ridges will be generalizations. However, a knowledgeable pilot will use his imagination and apply the correct principles to the situation at hand. The factors affecting lift on a ridge are its steepness, height, the presence of obstructions in front of it, the roughness of its slope, and, of course, the wind's velocity and angle to the ridge.

The higher the ridge (or mountain) and the steeper it is, the better the upward component and thus, the lift. In Figure 42 we see the effect of different shape slopes on the lift band. Note how the lift band extends further up and out on the cliff, while the slope exhibits usable lift further down the face. The area of best lift (indicated by the arrow) is at an angle away from the ridge as you rise higher. On the cliff this angle is not as great as it is on the slope. As the wind velocity changes, the size of the soarable envelope reduces, but the shape remains about the same.

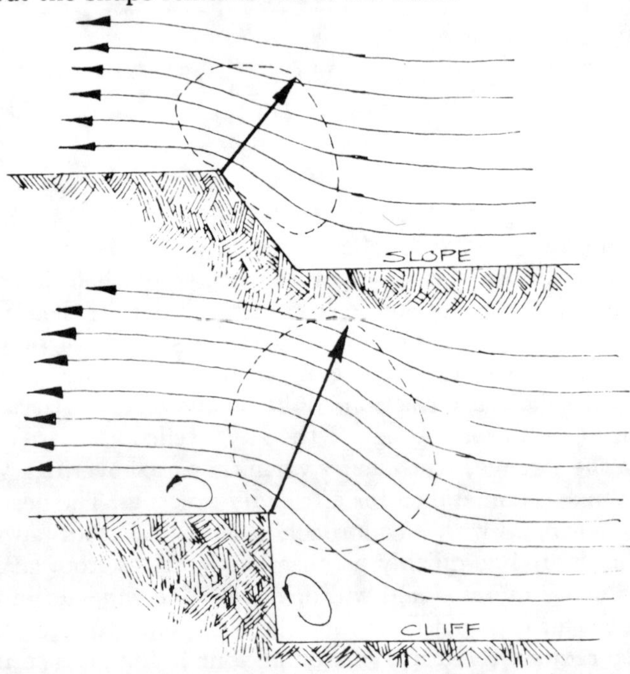

Figure 42 · Lift Patterns

Lift is where you find it in most cases. You must experiment, mentally record what you discover and explore the sky for better air. Eventually you will find the best place to gain height. Don't stay in one place – move around and look for elusive pockets of lift. "Parking" on a ridge offers a great view, but doesn't really teach you too much.

When the wind is perpendicular to a ridge, the lift is best. The slightest shift will result in less upward component. The steeper the ridge, the more sensitive the lift is to wind incidence angle. This explains why in shifty winds the lift on a cliff is so variable. You can be skyed out in one moment and be sinking out of the sky in the next, as the wind veers. On a slope, the change is not so dramatic. Use this knowledge to a good advantage. For instance, if you are soaring a ridge with a slight crosswind you may think the steepest part will get you highest. However, if the wind is cross too much you will find the gentler slope to produce more lift.

Smooth ridges – those covered with grass rather than trees and boulders – tend to produce better lift simply because they don't disrupt the wind flow as much in the lower layer. This is especially true in light winds (in stronger winds you quickly climb above the gradient layer).

Ridges with other ridges or mountains in front of them may have their lift destroyed or enhanced, depending on the conditions. Figure 43 shows a ridge whose lift is limited by the downmoving flow caused by the mountain upwind. If the upper air is stable, a wave may occur that will rebound just right to help build the lift on a ridge downwind from another ridge. Under this condition, a pilot will find himself in more lift than he would expect from a ridge working alone.

Figure 43 · Lift Interference

Waves can occur anywhere under the right conditions. These conditions are hard for a pilot to predict (see the book *Flying Conditions*), but he should recognize a wave when he enters one. The lift will be stronger than normal for the given wind velocity and the turbulence associated with thermals will be absent. To utilize wave lift, simply fly parallel to the ridge to stay in the upward moving air. A wave can be a changing, chimeral entity, so it may not be as easy as it sounds to stay in a wave. Since waves in the air occur a great percent of the time and are created by any solid object (even houses can set up small waves), the best flight plan is to treat wave lift like any lift source and explore the area for the best ride.

Another useful source of lift comes from the joining of upslope winds on different sides of a mountain as in Figure 44. These winds are caused by valley heating during the day. The area of lift over the mountain is properly called a "convergence zone." A hang glider pilot usually needs a few thermals or enough ridge lift on one side of the mountain in order to climb up to the useful lift in a convergence zone, but once he is there, he can float around all day in relatively smooth, easy comfort. To stay in the lift, simply stay over the mountain top. You can't miss!

A few words of caution are necessary for ridge riding pilots. First, the presence of waves introduce the possibility of shear turbulence. Not all waves are smooth. The inversion layers associated with wave conditions can exhibit turbulence. If winds are strong and a wave condition exists, you would be wise to stay low by flying away from the best lift (perpendicular to the ridge). There are times when pilots are caught in waves that take them higher than they want to go. These higher altitudes exhibit higher winds which may be too strong to penetrate into. A downwind run may be the worse choice in this situation as rotors associated with waves may be anywhere up to several miles behind the mountain. Such rotors may be hard to detect until you're in them. Airplanes have been downed in rotors.

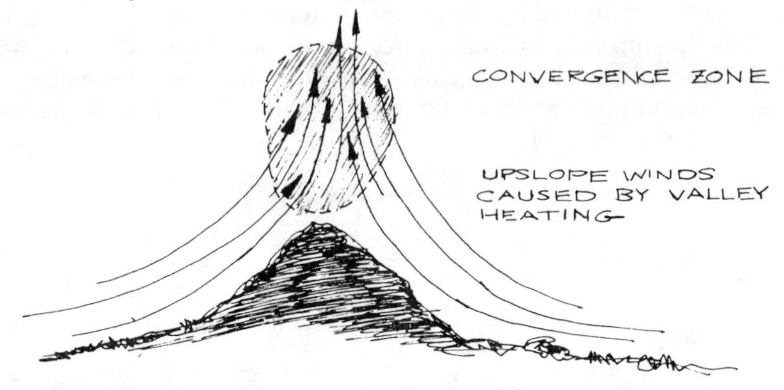

Figure 44 · Convergence Lift

Waves often set in at the end of a thermaly day. Be ready to circle down quickly if the wind picks up and the lift pegs your vario. Slipping turns will give you the greatest descent rate.

A second potential danger is the approach of cold fronts while the pilot is in the air. In Figure 45 we see a cold front approaching from the west creating super lift for the pilot soaring the easterly facing slope. As in a wave situation he may find himself in lift that is hard to leave. If the front gets too close he may encounter thunderstorms and suddenly shifting winds. To avoid this simply keep in touch with the general forecast (weathermen at least know where the fronts are) and keep an eye out for ominous sky in the west.

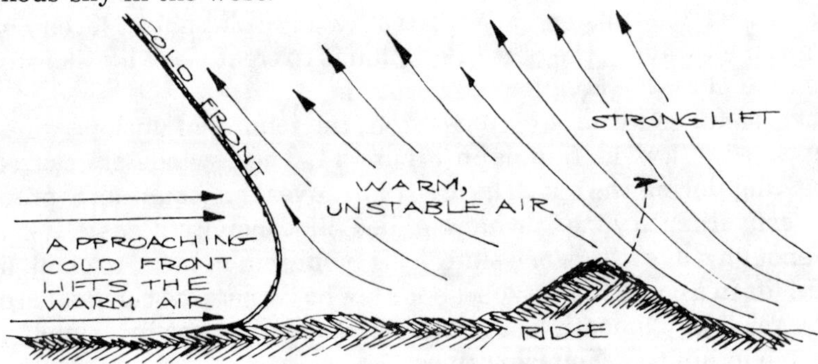

Figure 45 · Lift from a Cold Front

A convenient end to a ridge soaring flight is a landing on top. This trick can be risky if you don't know what you are doing. With trees and irregularities on the top of your ridge, you must be several hundred feet above the ridge so that you can travel downwind several hundred yards back from the edge to avoid rotors and turbulence. Even if you accomplish this, you may find the ride bumpy and the wind blowing in a strange direction in the top landing area. Wind streamers are a must in this case.

If your ridge is small and clear, or the top is rounded, you can land close to the edge since the airflow will be uniform. In this case you must be prepared to take off in the lift again if you overshoot. The proper approach for a top landing is shown in Figure 46. Note that the pilot flys parallel to the ridge, letting the wind drift him back over the top. When he is back far enough, he turns 90 ° to head into the wind and descend to a landing. If the landing area is limited, however, the pilot may have to drift downwind of the intended landing spot and S turn back and forth to lose the right amount of altitude to set up a proper landing. In either case, practice runs without actually landing can be made at several hundred feet above the ridge to get a feel for the amount of drift and penetration available.

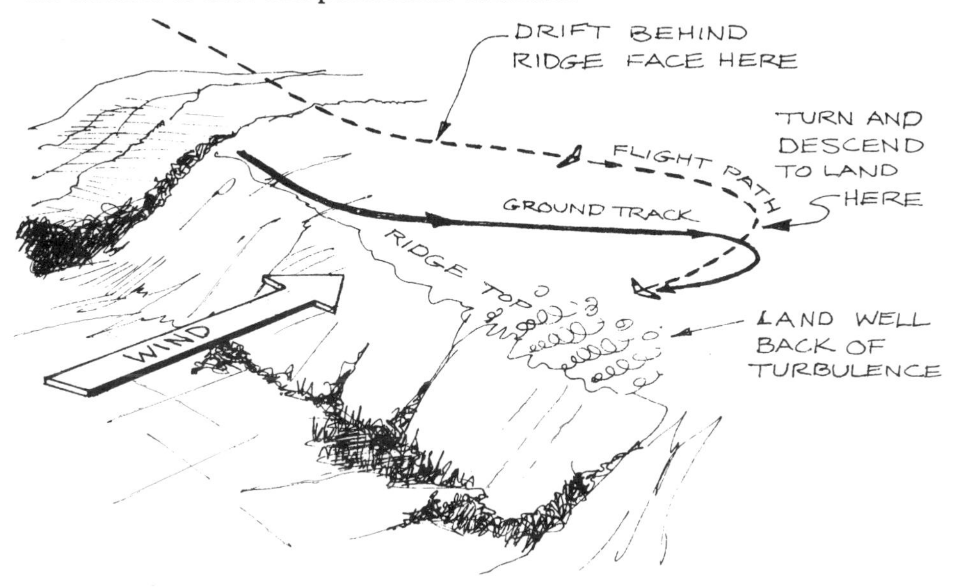

Figure 46 · Landing on Top

Remember, in the laminar (not rising) air over the top of a ridge you will have quite a steep descent path due to the strong headwind and lack of lift. Be sure to leave plenty of leeway for judgment error until you become quite experienced at top landing. Keep your airspeed up until you're about to touch down, then flare only a little to keep from rising again. Play with the pitch control to settle down gradually and gently. After landing on top, you can rest awhile then take off for another great soaring flight without even breaking your glider down.

CHAPTER V

THERMAL SOARING

One of the ultimate goals of hang glider pilots is learning to use thermal lift efficiently. Thermals can carry one higher and further than can pure ridge lift. In addition, thermals can sustain flight even on days when the wind is quite light. There is nothing better than gaining a couple thousand feet on a day when the wind barely puffs in at launch.

Learning to thermal requires time and practice. The rewards of a beautiful wandering flight high above the countryside are well worth the effort expended. The flying techniques involved in thermaling are somewhat different than those used in ridge soaring. In this chapter we will explore these techniques as well as the natural history of thermals in order to locate them most readily and use their lift most effectively. Since thermals are not visible, we need knowledge of their habits and a bit of imagination to increase the probability of utilizing their lift.

THE BIRTH OF A THERMAL

Thermals are children of the sun. The solar rays heat the ground, which in turn warms the overlying air. Air is not a good conductor of heat, so initially only the lower few feet are heated. If conditions are right, this layer of air will become quite warm and eventually break away from the ground to rise like a helium balloon. This mass of warm, rising air is called a thermal.

You can get an idea of the nature of thermal production by watching the formation of vapor bubbles in a plan of boiling water. These bubbles also cling to the bottom as they grow, then break away and float to the top. Notice how some of the bubbles grow larger and some rise faster than the others. What causes this action? The answer to this question applies equally to vapor bubbles in water and thermals.

When a patch of warm air is formed above a surface, the cooler air (or water) above presses downward as shown by the arrows in Figure 47a. This layer of warm air will expland as heating continues, until forces at the sides of the warm patch overcome the surface drag and gravity forces, and push in at the sides as shown in 47b. Cool air then rushes in below the warm patch as it begins to rise in a cohesive mass.

The air may rush in from all directions as the warm patch or thermal lifts off. This can be observed by placing wind indicators or streamers around a thermal-producing field. When the thermal is released, the streamers all point toward the center of the field (see Figure 48). The gusts we feel on a warm, sunny day are very often caused by the sudden rush of air as thermals break away. These conditions are known as light and variable.

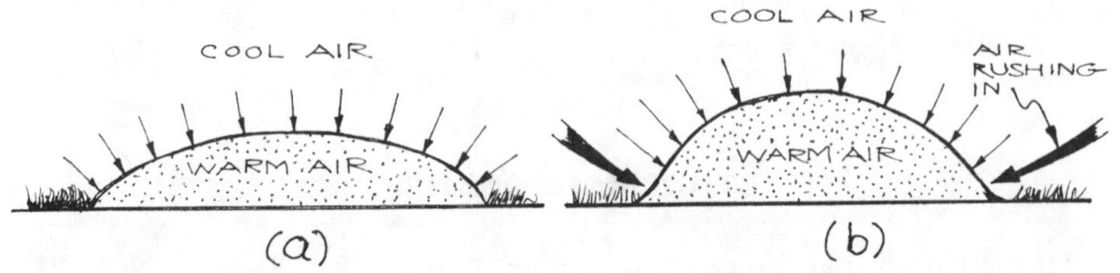

Figure 47 · Thermal Development

Of course, if a significant wind is present, the direction varies only slightly due to thermal activity, but very strong gusts related to sudden changes in wind speed will occur. Landings performed in these conditions are tricky at best. Remember, wind is a complicating factor in all flying.

Wind can prevent the build-up of large, strong thermals by causing them to release before too much air is heated. In fact, a strong wind will form a turbulent layer near the ground that continually mixes the air. As a result, the entire lower layer eventually becomes heated by the ground so that thermals release from some point above the surface in a random fashion. We will explore this interesting phenomenon in a later section.

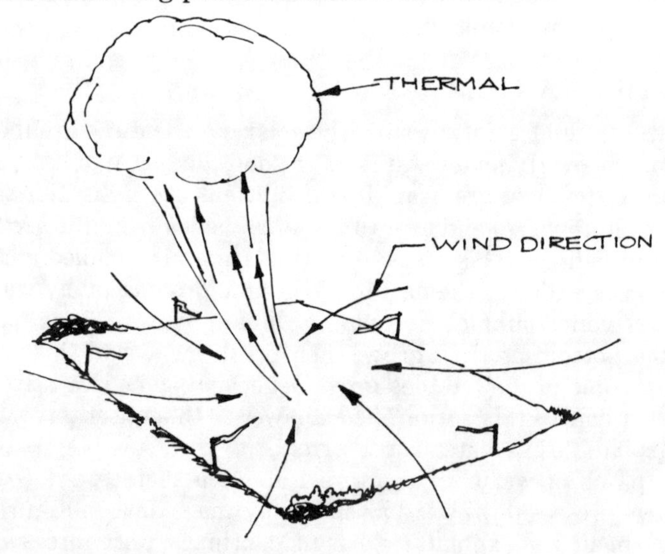

Figure 48 · Thermal Indicators

THERMAL SOURCES

Earlier, we mentioned the heating of the earth's surface as being the source of energy for thermals. It should be apparent that the more the sun heats a surface, the more readily it will produce a thermal. From this we can conclude that a slope tilted to face the sun, and areas where the sun's rays are strongest, (high altitude and cloudless regions) will be good thermal cookers. In addition, any surface that heats rapidly will be a good thermal generator. These surfaces include bare or plowed ground, fields of dry crops, parking lots and paved areas in general, buildings, rock outcroppings and slides, as well as benches.

Dry corn or weeds are exceptionally good since they heat a layer of air protected from the wind. In general, any area protected from wind, such as a field surrounded by trees or hills, will be an exceptional thermal source. In this case, a thermal may grow for up to half an hour before an errant breeze disturbs its brooding development. These large thermals release in one powerful surge and are quite workable due to their healthy size and strength. On the other hand, thermals developing on a plain exposed to the wind may pop off a given spot every few minutes.

Areas of poor thermal generation are those surfaces that dissipate the sun's heating: water, moist ground, snow and vegetation (grass and trees). Water evaporates, circulates and allows the sun's rays to penetrate deeply, which prevents the water's surface from heating too greatly. Moisture in the ground and vegetation also cool the surface by evaporation. Trees present a much greater surface area to distribute the heat, so the air remains cool in a forest.

Thermals do occur over water and forested areas at times, especially in the evening when the bare gound cools rapidly and the heat stored in the water and trees is released gradually in the form of weak thermals and convection. However, during daytime thermal activities, expect sink over these cooler expanses.

Since thermals will be found drifting downwind from a thermal source, or rising vertically in calm conditions, it is obvious that a successful thermal pilot will be the one who has learned how to judge his fields. To quote some pilots: "Thermals are where you find them." This means that there is no sure way to pinpoint exactly where that hot bubble is moving, but an educated guess is usually a good enough beginning.

THERMAL RISING

Once a thermal jumps off the ground, what keeps it rising? Look at Figure 49. Here we see a bubble surrounded by a fluid. The pressure on the bubble is indicated by the arrows pointing inward. Since pressure is caused by the weight of the surrounding fluid, it is clear that pressure increases as we go down, so the lower portion of the bubble receives more pressure. Thus, there is an unbalanced pressure force pushing the bubble upward. However, this force must overcome gravity pulling the bubble down. It should be easy to see that the lighter the bubble, the more it will want to rise. In fact, as long as the bubble is less dense than the surrounding fluid, the pressure difference will overcome the force of gravity since again, it is the weight of the surrounding fluid that causes the pressure at each level. Finally, we can see that if the bubble is a warm thermal surrounded by cooler, more dense air, it will rise.

From high school physics we recall that a gas expands when pressure around it is reduced. Also, as this gas expands, it cools (the same amount of heat energy becomes spread throughout a greater volume). Consequently, when a thermal is lifted it expands and cools due to the lowered pressure (remember that air pressure decreases as one rises). Now, if this bubble remains warmer than the surrounding air, it will continue to rise. If, however, the bubble becomes cooler than the surrounding air, it will stop its ascent and float along at the level where its temperature equals that of the surrounding air. We should now see that the rate of a thermal's rise is determined not by its size, but by how warm it is compared to the surrounding air.

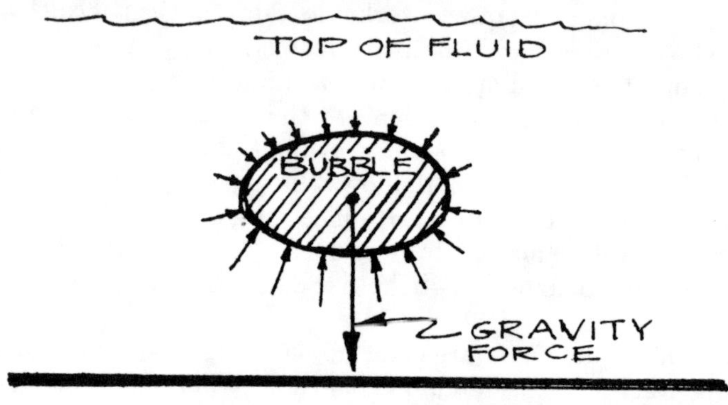

Figure 49 · Bubble Rising in a Fluid

Through experiment we know that a portion of dry air in the atmosphere will cool 5½ °F per 1,000 feet (3 °C/300 m). Thus, a dry thermal rising a thousand feet will cool 5½ °F. It is easy to see that if the surrounding air drops off in temperature an amount greater than 5½ °F/1,000 ft., the thermal will continue to rise since it will always be warmer than the surrounding air. Conversely, if the surrounding air temperature drops less than 5½ °F/1,000 ft., at some point the thermal will become cooler than the surrounding air and upward motion will stop.

The 5½ °F/1,000 ft. critical value is called the Dry Adiabatic Lapse Rate (DALR). Lapse rate is simply the amount of drop in temperature as altitude is gained. If the lifting air (thermal) is moist, the critical lapse rate becomes somewhat different since some of the water vapor will condense as it cools and release its heat of vaporization. In this case, the critical lapse rate is between 2 ° and 5 °F per 1,000 ft. (1.1 to 2.8 °C/300 m) and is called the Moist Adiabatic Lapse (MALR).

The lapse rate in the air is not constant with altitude or time. The cooling effects of the surface at night and heating during the day cause a diurnal variation. Air masses changing over the land also drastically alter the lapse rate profile over a given spot. Figure 50 shows a few typical lapse rates. This is simply a graph depicting how the air's temperature changes as altitude is gained. Note the presence of an inversion layer in the first graph. This is a layer where the air's temperature actually increases as altitude is gained. With a little thought, we can see that a thermal would have a hard time rising in an inversion layer, since the surrounding air actually gets warmer as the thermal rises.

A layer of air that does not cool enough with altitude is known as a stable layer. Likewise, unstable air is that which is conducive to thermal production. It is quite easy to measure the lapse rate and thus stability of the air with a thermometer and an altimeter. However, most pilots don't take such pains since the stability of the air can be foretold by other means. These include sudden ground gusts, the presence of thermaling raptors (hawks, eagles, vultures, etc.), the development of cumulus clouds and a marked drop in temperature as you drive up to the launch site.

Although it's important to understand the mechanism of thermals, an experienced pilot does not need to carry meteorological instruments around to know what the air is doing. This is where imagination and intuition enter the picture. After years of watching the wind and assessing the air and the currents, a pilot develops a sixth sense for telling where and when thermals exist.

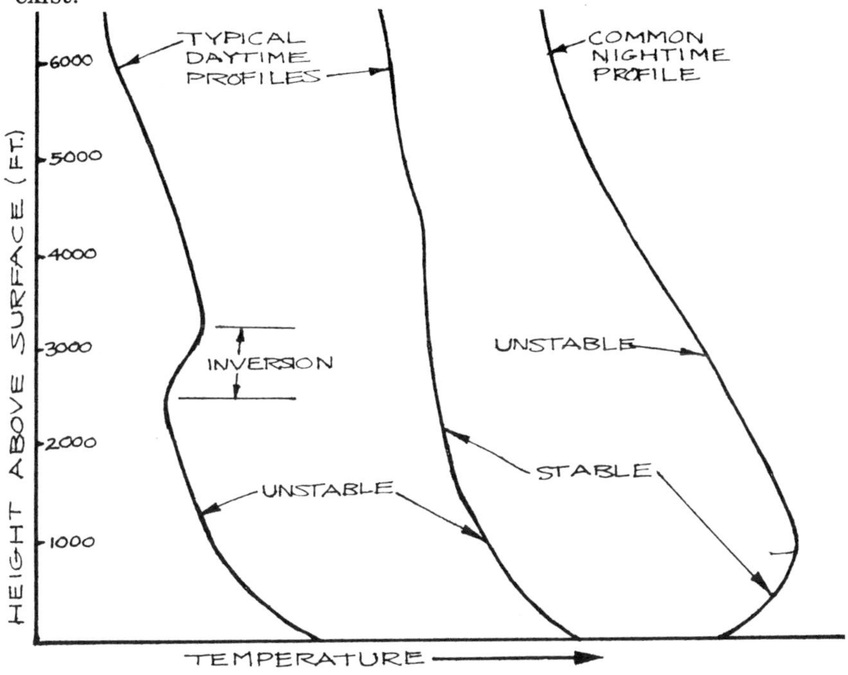

Figure 50 · Typical Lapse Rates

THE THERMAL LIFE CYCLE

We can separate a thermal's history into three stages. These are:

STAGE I: The thermal is "born" from a heated layer of air on the surface that contracts to form a bubble and begins to rise quite rapidly, picking up speed until its drag slows it down. Thermals in this stage tend to be strong and turbulent, as can be attested to by pilots who have entered a thermal as low as 50 feet above the ground and worked it skyward.

The thermal contracts initially as it assumes a spherical shape, then expands fairly constantly with height. The maximum velocity a thermal reaches depends on two things – its size (radius) and its buoyancy. It is found that larger thermals rise faster than smaller ones if all other factors are the same. The size of the thermal mainly depends on the size of the surface from which it originated. Isolated thermals can range in size from a few feet to several thousand feet. If less than sixty feet in diameter, a thermal will probably be of little use since the strength will be low and it will be difficult to remain in the lift.

The buoyancy is determined by the difference in heating of the thermal and the surrounding air, as mentioned above. This is a function of the lapse rate, and again, the nature of the heating surface. If a good thermal ground source is protected from the wind by trees, hills or some other solid object, it will tend to heat the air above it for a longer period of time before the thermal bubble breaks away and floats upward. A thermal produced under these circumstances will be very strong since it will be much warmer than the surrounding air. On the other hand, a wind-swept field will produce weaker and smaller thermals at a faster rate than the "protected" field. Only a very shallow layer of air can be heated in the latter case, as the wind constantly triggers the thermal release. In general, a calm day will exhibit larger and more powerful thermals.

STAGE II: The thermal has consolidated, but slows more and more as it grows larger and erodes away. This is the state of thermal development in which most flying takes place. If the thermal is strong, the pilot will be able to rise into the top of the core and continue upward, enclosed within the bubble (see Figure 51). On the other hand, if the thermal is weak, at some point the upward moving air (lift) may not be able to sustain the glider since the thermal itself slows its ascent rate, even though it continues to rise. This second stage may begin as high as 300 feet above the thermal generating surface, but is usually lower.

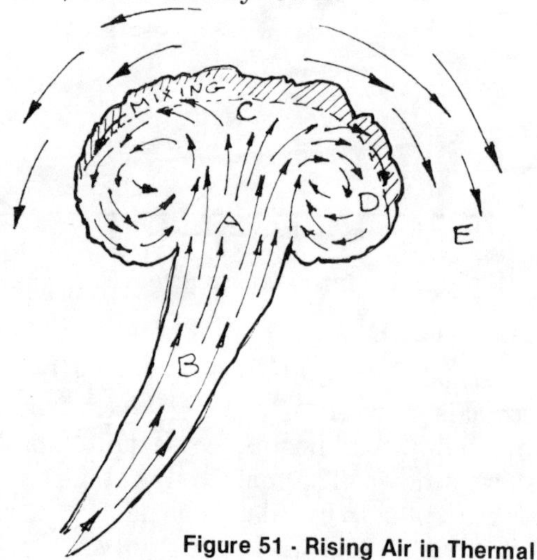

Figure 51 · Rising Air in Thermal

STAGE III: The thermal dissipates from one or more causes. To understand this process, we must understandd the mechanisms of both cloud formation and inversions. When a thermal rises, it may carry moisture aloft in the form of water vapor. This moisture cools along with the thermal as the whole màss rises. Eventually, the water vapor is cooled to the point that condensation occurs. When this happens, small water droplets form and are seen as clouds. In addition, the "energy of vaporization" is released into the air which greatly increases the thermal's buoyancy. The sudden surge of energy into the relatively small thermal volume results in great mixing which effectively dilutes the thermal with cool surrounding air. This dilution along with the sudden change of water vapor to water droplets quickly decreases the buoyancy of the thermal and stops its rise. This process is illustrated in Figure 52. Note how the thermal stops in a cloud even though the lapse rate continues to be favorable. The dew point is the temperature at which the water vapor condenses.

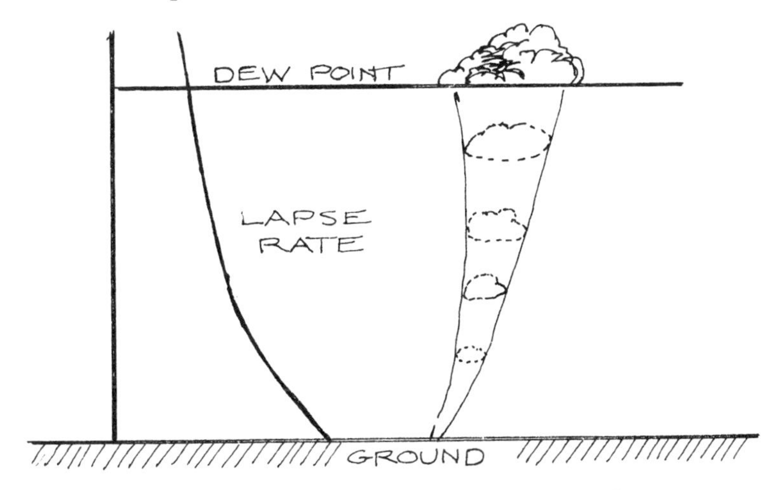

Figure 52 · Thermal Ending in Cumulus Cloud

Since the temperature aloft is fairly constant over a wide area, all the thermal-produced cumulus clouds have bases at the same altitude. Cumulus clouds are the individual puffy clouds that look like cotton floating in the blue sky. The presence of these clouds is one of the signs of thermal activity.

The second cause of a thermal's dissipation is an inversion layer. As explained before, an inversion exists when the air actually gets warmer at some altitude. When the thermal meets this layer, it may slow down or stop rising since it only remains buoyant if it is warmer than the surrounding air (see Figure 53).

Inversion layers are common in the upper levels. Often, they are accompanied by turbulence produced by shear action (layers moving with different velocities) and the breaking apart of thermals. When moist thermals are arrested in an inversion layer, the relative humidity of the layer gradually builds up until strato-cumulus clouds (puffy layer-type) form. The development of such a cloud layer may effectively block the sun's heating and shut off the thermal activity. This state of affairs is known as "overdevelopment," or O.D.

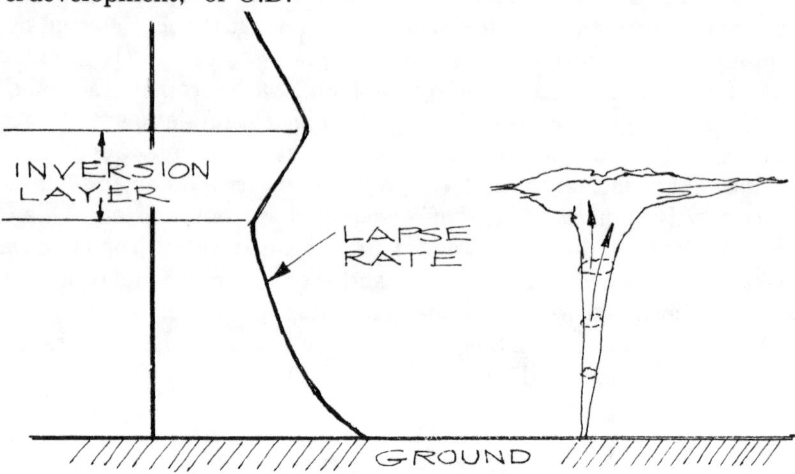

Figure 53 - Thermal Ending in Inversion Layer

In addition, the heat the thermals carry aloft is dispersed throughout the inversion layer making it thicker and more pronounced. Thus, the maximum height that can be gained in a thermal may become lower as the day wears on. On the other hand, if thermals are ending in cumulus clouds, the cloudbase may become higher as the heat carried aloft rises the dew point to a greater altitude.

Occasionally, a thermal meeting an inversion will have enough momentum to punch through and continue to rise in unstable air above the inversion. In this case, the thermal will meet its end as in Figure 52, or dwindle as explained below.

The third and final way a thermal dissipates is to simply melt away. As the thermal rises, it expands and creates more drag as it tries to push upward. Also it mixes with the surrounding air as it progresses. Gradually, this mixing cools the thermal so that it dies a quiet death. When no moisture is present, a thermal is known as a "blue" or "dry" thermal. A blue thermal rising in an atmosphere free of an inversion will gradually erode away as shown in Figure 54. Even a moist thermal will undergo this process if it is weak and slows before it meets the dew point.

THE IDEAL THERMAL

In our discussion to this point, we have considered our thermals to be well formed and well behaved with a single core and uniform shape. We call this nice bubble an ideal thermal. There is plenty of evidence that ideal thermals do exist in nature a certain percentage of the time, especially in the lower reaches where hang glider pilots are apt to meet them. Experiments with smoke generators and sodium solutions in water provide a good picture of an ideal thermal's behavior and form. For an ideal thermal to exist, there must be uniform heating throughout the thermal mass (determined by the uniformity of the surface forming the thermal), light or negligible wind, fairly consistent lapse rate and good separation of thermal sources.

Learning the techniques for working an ideal thermal comes first, so let's draw a picture. In Figure 51, we see an ideal thermal rising in the free air. The arrows indicate the air flow. The longer the arrows, the faster the movement. From the figure, we can see that the fastest vertical movement and thus the greatest lift is in the center (A). We call this the core and unlike the core of an apple, it is the thermal's best part.

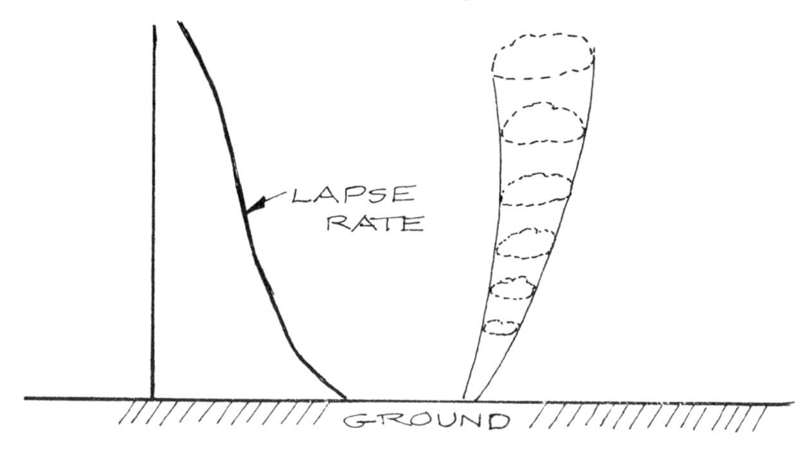

Figure 54 · Dissipation of Blue Thermal

As the core rises it spreads out at the top of the thermal, moves out to the sides, down, then towards the center for another round. The whole thermal is constantly turning itself inside out like a smoke ring. Due to this "vortex ring" action, the entire thermal only rises about half as fast as the upward flow in the core.

A pilot positioned at A or B in Figure 51 will rise at the rate of the upward flow minus his craft's sink rate. If the upward flow is sufficiently strong, he will rise rapidly into the thermal to point C, at which time his upward progress slows to the rate of the thermal as a whole. A pilot flying at point D would find much less lift than at either of the previous three positions (despite the downward point arrows, the air is not necessarily sinking at D since the entire thermal is moving upward). A glider at E, however, is in sinking air surrounding the thermal. This cooler air is usually sinking most vigorously on the downwind side.

In addition to the up and down air, a thermal also exhibits general areas of turbulence. These are the areas of mixing along the top and sides of the thermal. Often, a sudden surge of lift is encountered when passing from the sinking air around the thermal to the lifting air inside. This sudden lift may be very abrupt or barely noticeable, depending on the thermal intensity. The possibility of multiple cores are additional sources of rollicking air.

THE REAL THERMAL

It should be clear from the above that even an ideal thermal can be quite boisterous. If a fresh wind is blowing, the thermal will be less uniform and more turbulent as the flow gets blown around. The presence of wind will cause the thermal to drift and tilt as shown in Figure 55. This further complicates the matter of finding and following the thermal core.

More often than not, a real thermal will have multiple cores, or at least several areas of strong lift. This is caused by the action of wind as well as the joining of two or more thermals. If the wind is really vigorous, the patches of lift will vary constantly and be quite turbulent. Often, the disturbance created by one thermal releasing or passing overhead may trigger the release of another thermal. These thermals then join together to form a larger, more vigorous thermal with multiple cores.

Figure 55 · Drifting Thermal

At times, the air overlying a large area on the surface may become heated to the point of instability. If a light surface breeze is blowing, this air may move along until it meets a hill or slight rise which starts the air mass moving upwards. In this case, a column thermal results, being continuously fed by the unlimited supply of air at the surface. This is illustrated in Figure 56.

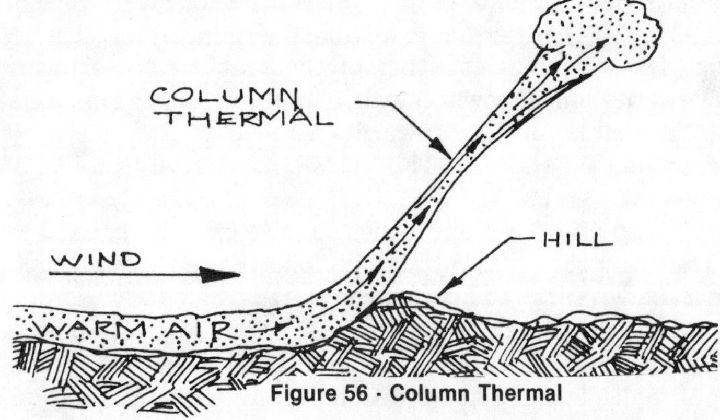

Figure 56 · Column Thermal

Another important thermal phenomenon is cloud streets. This refers to the lining up of thermals in the direction of the wind like rows of soldiers with curious white hats. Cloud streets occur during specific conditions (a strong wind gradient, about a 15 mph wind and an inversion aloft), but are actually quite commonly observed. Generally, areas of great lift occur under the rows of clouds, while insidious sink lurks between the rows. Figure 57 shows a typical cloud street pattern.

When flying cloud streets, it is desirous to stay under the row of lift, so a downwind path is usually taken to achieve the most distance. Of course, if your launch site is between rows, you are probably out of luck since the streets can be spaced as much as several miles apart. Be aware that on a dry day, thermals and streets may exist without the telling presence of clouds. In this case, they are called "blue streets" and "blue thermals." For more information on these and other types of thermal forms, see *Flying Conditions* by this author.

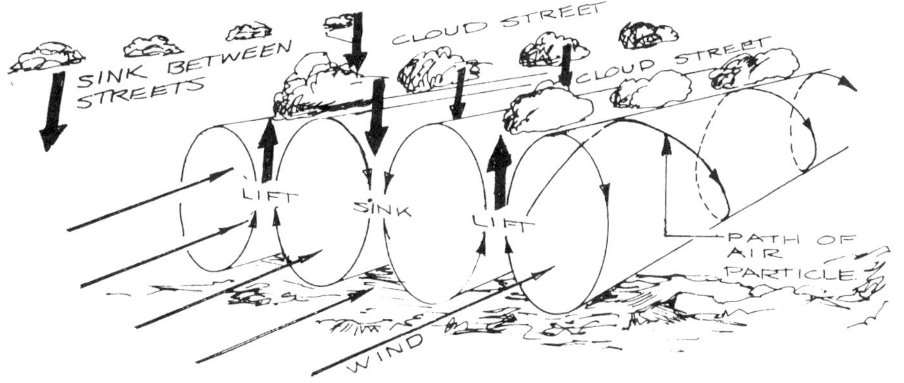

Figure 57 - Cloud Street Formations

LOCATING THE LIFT

In an earlier section, we indicated the type of ground cover conducive to thermal formation. This turns out to be material that is easily heated by the sun, such as pavement, dried crops, plowed fields, sand and rock surfaces. Naturally, the best thermal hunting is somewhere above these areas.

In a calm wind, a thermal will be straight up from the ground source. However, the wind is rarely calm during the midday thermal-production hours, so we have to imagine how the thermals drift with the wind. Figure 56 shows a column thermal formed when a continuous warm air source meets a hill or slope. It should be clear that finding the lift in this case requires searching downwind of the apparent ground source. The higher you are, the further downwind you must be.

In Figure 58, we see a pulsating thermal source (the thermals are released one after another as the air above the ground source heats up). In this case, the lift is again located downwind from the thermal release point.

When surface winds are strong, thermals may not form at any singular source, since there is a constant change of air. However, the entire layer of air above the ground can become unstable. This layer is usually quite turbulent. A thermal born in this situation will move along with the wind, but will exhibit an almost vertical column or tail since it will be constantly fed by the layer of unstable air. This is shown in Figure 59. In this case, a pilot must fly directly under the thermal to utilize the lift. Of course, he/she must still drift along with the wind. As we shall see, there is a slightly different technique necessary for taking advantage of the lift in a vertical column and a slanting column.

Figure 58 · Pulsating Thermal

Using a ground reference to locate thermal lift is usually only useful in about the lower thousand feet since the change in wind velocity and direction, as well as the variation of the thermal's vertical velocity, makes prediction of the thermal's track quite difficult. However, the presence of birds or gliders at various altitudes are good cues to indicate where the lift is and how much drift occurs at their altitude. Occasionally, we can get a good idea of a thermal's path from the ground source all the way to cloudbase.

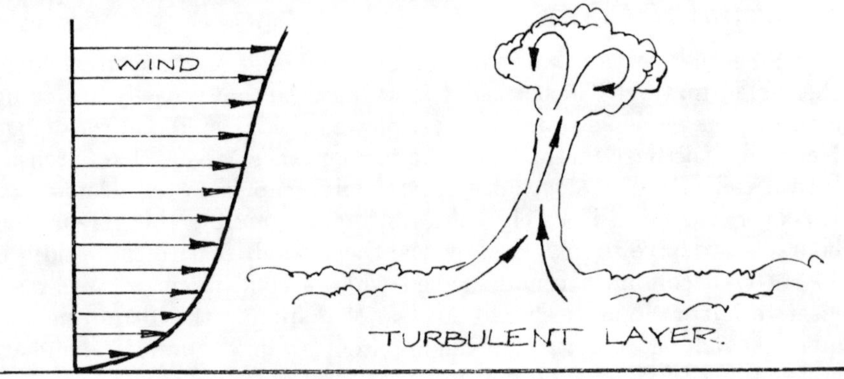

Figure 59 · Thermal Rising from Turbulent Layer

As we rise higher in a thermal, we should become less dependent upon ground references and more dependent upon the positions of clouds and our instruments. At times, only our sense of feel and our vario can give us any input regarding the location of lift. At higher altitudes – just below cloudbase, for example – we can rely on the clouds to indicate the areas of lift. The darkest areas of a cloud are the spots being fed most vigorously by thermals or individual cores. In addition, the upwind side of a cloud will usually exhibit the best lift.

The life cycle of a thermal-dependent cumulus cloud is shown in Figure 60. At first, small wisps appear as the moist thermal reaches the condensation level. Later, a well-defined "cotton ball' is formed that may begin eroding on the downwind side. This erosion increases until nothing but sink exists in the vicinity of the cloud. By the time the cloud reaches the stage represented by the third drawing, it may be too late to find any useful lift.

Figure 60 · Life Cycle of Thermal Cloud

CONVECTIVE BARRIERS

Cloudbase is not necessarily the limit of climb in thermal conditions. When a large, warm mass of upward moving air continues to rise into faster moving air, the horizontal velocity of the warm mass is always somewhat slower than that of the surrounding air. This is because the air from below starts out slower (remember, the wind usually slows near the surface) and possesses inertia so the upper winds see the warm mass as a barrier. The upper winds must then lift over or go around this "convective barrier."

Figure 61 shows a typical case of lift created in ront of (upwind) and above a large cloud formation. Sink is usually expected on the downwind side of this large cloud. If thermals feed this cloud on a more or less continuous basis from a stationary ground source, the cloud itself will remain in about

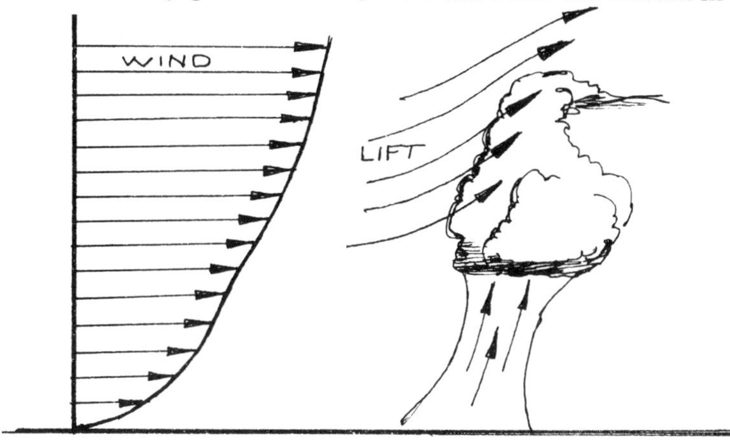

Figure 61 · Lift from a Convective Barrier

the same place (growing in front and eroding downwind) and act like a hill creating continuous orographic lift.

The technique to use when exploiting this type of lift is to soar back and forth in front of the cloud just as if you were riding a ridge. Occasionally, the air will move around the cloud, converge behind and well up just as it does on an isolated hill. This convergence behind the cloud cannot be depended on, so head to the front of the cloud if a choice is available.

As a word of caution, avoid flying into the cloud. This is illegal as well as dangerous (disorientation and severe turbulence can result). Also, you should observe the FAA rules regarding clearance from the limits of clouds. If you find yourself climbing the wall of a towering cloud, watch for traffic, enjoy the view and give thanks.

THERMALS ON A RIDGE

Much of hang gliding thermal flying takes place on a ridge or above a mountain. The reasons for this are: 1) A pilot often has to ridge soar (using lift created by the upward deflected air) until a thermal drifts through, especially if his site is less than a thousand feet above the valley. 2) The ridges and mountains collect thermals as they drift along on the wind. Hang gliders don't have the performance to search a wide area for thermals, so the much greater abundance of thermals along a ridge is of significance. 3) Mountain slopes tend to produce more thermals than valleys since the slope may face directly into the sun and the slope's surface can be heated to a greater temperature with respect to the surrounding air, since air at higher elevations is initially cooler than air in the valleys.

Now, every experienced pilot knows that if we fly along a ridge for any length of time we will eventually blunder into a thermal. However, it is much more profitable to seek certain areas that have a high probability of containing a thermal. From preceding discussion, it should be clear that a position on the ridge downwind from a good thermal-producing field is an ideal place to be. Also, bowls or spines on the ridge may heat better or concentrate th airflow to gather more thermals. Rocks or bare areas on the slopes will often continuously generate their own thermals. Finally, an area on a ridge showing much activity such as rustling or swaying of leaves and branches will invariably be under the influence of a thermal.

A "house thermal" is an area of lift produced by a continuous thermal or individual thermals released in succession. A house thermal usually is associated with a unique feature of the terrain, such as the top of a bowl or a rock pile. Once you find a house thermal on a ridge or mountain, you can usually depend on its lift. However, when the lift diminishes, move out of the area and return a bit later. Chances are the house thermal will again be pumping. With a little observation and experimentation you can learn to perceive the pace of the lift cycles on any given day.

LAUNCHING INTO THERMALS

In special cases, the approach of a thermal can be detected from launch by noting its progressive disturbance of trees or brush. When the wind is light, timing a takeoff to become airborne just as a thermal passes may be the only chance of soaring on a particular day. Take time to observe the length of the lift cycle, the duration between thermals, the speed of progress of the thermal and the increase in wind velocity as the thermal passes. From these observations you can determine the proper launch timing.

If the thermals are small and strong, it's best to launch ahead of their arrival so that you are clear of the hill before their associated turbulence hits. If the thermals are strong but large, take off just as their leading edge passes and utilize the best lift in the core to climb above launch quickly. If weak thermals are all you get, launch just before they reach you so that you can exploit their full extent.

The worst turbulence and downdrafts associated with a thermal tend to be around the perimeter. Thus, launching into the leading or trailing portion of a thermal can be risky since handling rowdy air requires maneuvering room. Many a pilot has been rocked and rolled by a rebellious thermal right after launch. With a little observation and good timing you can avoid such borderline flying.

The trail of a thermal is left by the tail of the thermal picking up unstable air as it progresses up the slope, or the rolling action of the thermal itself as it encounters the mountain face. In no instance should the above discussion be misconstrued to be condoning launches into a dust devil. Dust devils are columns of madly spinning air created when a thermal rips away from the ground in very unstable conditions. Flying into a dust devil with a hang glider at any altitude can be deadly. When dust devils abound, time their frequency and launch well clear of their position. Meet the thermals that are kicking up the dust devils away from the hill so you have plenty of control options.

DETECTING THERMALS

One of the most important aspects of thermal flying is locating the thermal in the first place, then subsequently determining the extent of the lifting area. As indicated, a pilot can rely heavily on the physical senses when close enough to the ground (or other pilots) to detect vertical motion. However, a variometer is an invaluable asset when flying above 1,000 feet or so, or in light thermals at any altitude. The consummate pilot will use both instruments and senses in a complimentary manner to exploit thermals effectively.

The sense of feel is an important asset when thermal flying. Often, the warmth of a thermal compared to the surrounding air will serve to indicate when one is inside the bubble. More readily detectable is the turbulence and surge of lift encountered when passing into a thermal. Very often, an abrupt lifting of a glider's nose or tilting of the wings will occur as the pilot flies into the thermal. Occasionally, a series of hard bumps announces the thermal's boundary, giving way to smooth air inside the bubble. On the other hand, large, weak thermals may exhibit no turbulence whatsoever, but deliver gradually increasing lift.

Once inside a thermal and heading for the core, a pilot can often feel the G forces associated with a change in vertical motion. A strong thermal will cause a great tug on the harness straps. A pilot may feel like a yo-yo in heavy thermal conditions. The problem with trying to use this sense exclusively, is that gradual changes may not be detected, and continuous lift (or sink) will not be felt since the upward force on the body returns to one G (the force of gravity) when upward motion is neither increasing or decreasing. However, since the body also feels a reduction in G forces when lift is reduced, an overall picture of a thermal's extent can be deduced by this method in well-defined thermal conditions. As an experiment, try riding in a car on a hilly road with your eyes closed. Have the driver keep a steady speed and see if you can tell him or her when you are going up, down, or level, simply by feeling the change in G forces. The slower the car moves, the harder it will be to judge the ups and downs, similar to the case of large, weak thermals. Obviously, this technique is limited by the insensitivity of the human body, but the principle is very accurate when employed in inertial guidance systems.

When exiting a thermal, turbulence and sink are again commonly experienced. This time, the nose often drops as it enters downward moving air, or air with considerably less upward motion than the bulk of the thermal. A severe case of this nose-dropping, tail-lifting, diving syndrome is known as "going over the falls." Most thermal pilots can attest to the accuracy of this expression.

The sense of smell is a useful indicator of a thermal's presence. Very often, a thermal will carry aloft the odors present on the ground where the thermal originated. I have personally thermaled without instruments over a large farm by sniffing for cows, as well as over a construction site guided by the scent of tar.

By far, the most important sense is sight. In the same way that odors are carried aloft when a thermal rises, so too are leaves, paper and other debris. Occasionally, a floating bit of trash is encountered in a thermal. More reliable is the practice of keying on birds and other pilots. Soaring birds have an uncanny ability to locate the best thermals with the best cores, so join them. They certainly will rush into your thermal if they see you outclimbing them. The presence of another pilot almost doubles the area of aerial exploration. You can watch other gliders and see the lift or sink they encounter just as readily as flying through it yourself. However, be aware of the fact that many times when another pilot appears to be rising in lift, you are actually sinking (and vice versa). Still, his or her position is at least better than yours.

One of the most important visual clues to the presence of thermals is cumulus clouds. As we saw above, these clouds are, in fact, formed by thermals. Only when a pilot is approaching say a thousand feet below the base of the clouds can they be used to judge the location of thermals. Thermals drift with the wind. If the wind velocity at various altitudes is unknown, it's hard to estimate the path of a thermal feeding the cloud. However, the best hunting grounds below a cumulus cloud are usually upwind.

When flying at lower altitudes (3,000 feet AGL or less), the best place to be is downwind from potential ground sources of thermals (dry fields, rocks, buildings, etc.). Sometimes, a direct relationship between ground sources and clouds can be established, especially in light winds. The obvious choice is to fly between the two.

Of course, thermals can be present when cumulus clouds are absent. We call these "blue thermals." In addition, layers of air lifted to the point of instability will produce a regular pattern of cumulus or strato-cumulus clouds. These clouds represent convection (or Bernard) cells with usable lift, but they are usually above the reach of terrain-launching hang glider pilots.

The final visual clue is the thermal "tail." When a thermal lifts off, surrounding air rushes in to replace the lifting air. Very often, this rushing air is itself unstable and will follow the thermal aloft. As the thermal moves along in the wind, it may trigger the release of other thermals, so that the net effect is a continuous disturbance along the ground, tracing the progress of the thermal.

Generally, the position of the thermal will be downwind of the ground disturbance, as in Figure 62, position A. However, my experience as well as that of others I have interviewed is that above the ridge, the "tail" tends to be ahead of the thermal. In the East, where trees cover the ridges, it is common to see branches swaying and leaves rustling as a thermal passes through. When flying on top of a ridge and spotting such a disturbance on the slope, often we find the lift upwind or away from the ridge with respect to the disturbance. My theory (I have found no literature on the subject) explaining this phenomenon is that the thermal "tail" gets accelerated ahead

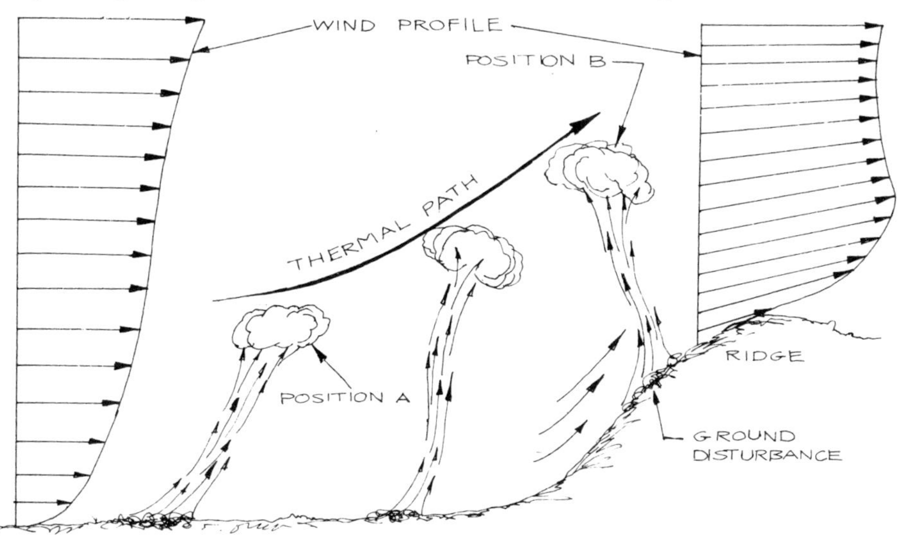

Figure 62 · Thermal Lift on a Ridge

of the main body by the upslope (anabatic) circulation as well as the venturi effect caused by the ridge. This action is illustrated in Figure 62, position B. Note the wind profile at the different positions.

The final visual clue to a thermal's presence is a dust devil. In reality, a dust devil is a specialized case of the "tail" described above. If the lapse rate is exceptionally strong, a thermal will lift off quickly, bringing fast moving air in to replace the thermal. If this air has some rotation (vorticity) – as it invariably does – it will rotate very rapidly as it draws together, similar to the swirling of water going down a bathtub drain. This rapid swirling kicks up dust and debris with devilish impunity.

In general, a thermal will be above or downwind of a dust devil when the thermal is low. However, since a dust devil doesn't travel strictly downwind due to its rotation (similar to a "curve" ball thrown with spin), at some point the thermal and dust devil part company. A thermal will be to the right of a clockwise rotating dust devil when viewed in the upwind direction. Dust devils *do* rotate both ways in the northern hemisphere, although clockwise may be their preferred direction due to Coriolis effect.

Below we shall look at the dangers of flying near dust devils. For now, it is sufficient to say that the presence of a dust devil belies the presence of a thermal. With experience, thermals based on dust devils can be located quite readily.

LEARNING TO THERMAL

To utilize thermal lift, you must stay within the confines of the thermal. If the thermal is small, this means circling continuously like a hawk. Being able to perform continuous smooth 360° turns is the most important skill needed for successful thermal flying. Performing 360° turns can be a problem on a ridge. The "backside" of the turn is downwind and aimed at the ridge. If the wind is strong, you may find yourself approaching the ridge at a high rate of speed.

The best policy for avoiding unnecessary risks is to only attempt a full 360 in strong winds if you have a minimum of 200 feet altitude above the ridge. In very light winds, you complete a circle with much less clearance. Here's how to go about learning to circle safely on a ridge: first, practice the turns on a day without thermals. Concentrate only on producing a smooth continuous 360 and seeing how much you drift into the ridge. Allow plenty of clearance at first, then bring the turns in closer to the ridge as your judgment becomes more precise. You can't practice this in light winds without thermals, since the ridge won't be soarable.

The next step is to practice your turns on a light thermal day. The procedure for all pilots to follow is to ride the ridge until a thermal is encountered, then perform 180° turns back and forth until the thermal has disappeared. If you are successful at this a few times you will have enough height to go looking for your first real thermal ride.

The next step is to fly away from the ridge at an angle until you encounter a convenient thermal. You should now be away from the ridge and a good bit above it. As soon as you enter it, wait for it to build then start your turn towards the ridge. If you perform properly, you will rise and stay in the thermal as it drifts toward the ridge. You may be able to turn several times before you are over the ridge top. Caution: at this point, do not go beyond the top of the ridge. Practice this technique in varying wind conditions and thermal strengths. Eventually, you will be able to work the elusive thermals like a raptor.

Although learning to work thermals sounds easy, there are a few more tricks involved. Turbulence is one of the big problems. To fly thermals you must be able to handle turbulence. Often when you are turning you will fly into the rolling edge of the thermal and get tipped into a steeper bank. You must be ready to maintain your equilibrium with quick correcting responses. After many hours in thermal conditions, you will feel relaxed and use your judgment most effectively.

The big decision in most thermal flying is: how tight to circle. The steeper you bank, the smaller the radius of your turn, but the greater your sink rate. You must bank steeper to stay in small, strong cores, but at some point staying close to the core will do no good if too steep a bank is required. There is a law of diminishing returns operating here. In general, 20 ° to 30 ° bank angles are in order for the majority of thermals. Occasionally, a strong localized core will require a circle with a 45 ° bank in order to maximize upward velocity. At times, even a 60 ° bank can be applied for brief intervals to rapidly hook an elusive, tight pop of lift.

The secret in all cases is to simply achieve the greatest climb rate in whatever lift distribution you encounter. As you may guess, a variometer is a great assistant for this purpose. However, practice without a vario is useful indeed, since one of the most important thermal skills is performing smooth, continuous turns and judging where you are in relation to a core.

One very useful trick when entering a thermal is counting a few seconds before starting to turn. The experienced pilot is well familiar with the days when thermals are encountered everywhere but are too small to utilize. It is often said that counting to three before turning is optimum. At 20 mph, this three-second delay will measure out almost 90 feet. This is a decent size thermal for a bank of 30 ° since flying at 20 mph in a 30 ° bank describes a circle with about a 94-foot diameter. However, for stronger cores or smaller thermals, a two-second delay with a 45 ° bank is appropriate. This latter bank angle at 20 mph results in a 54-foot diameter circle. With practice, it becomes easy to judge the optimum place to begin turning in a thermal to stay in the best lift.

Often, a thermal is encountered with one wing only. The classic method of grabbing the thermal (according to sailplane technique) is to perform a 270 ° turn away from the lifted wing as shown in Figure 63, path A. Since the turn is already started to the right, the pilot simply continues around to enter the thermal head on. However, with the current crop of fast-turning hang gliders, it is most expedient to overcome the force of the thermal lifting the near wing, and turn 90 ° directly into the thermal as shown by the dashed lines (path B).

Which way should you circle a thermal? Assuming that you are equally proficient at turning in both directions (which you should be), turn in the direction you started when entering the thermal. However, be aware that most thermals have multiple cores and the lift can change on the way up. Birds rarely turn in one direction more than ten circles (usually less), so learn to hunt like a hawk for the best lift even if it means breaking stride and circling the other way.

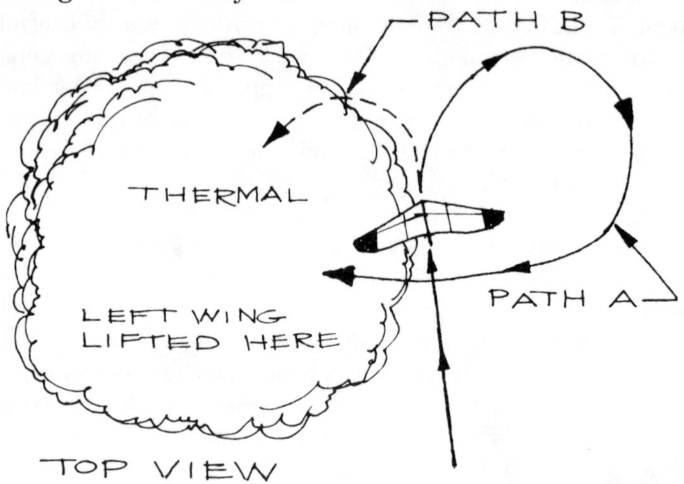

Figure 63 · Entering a Thermal

One other consideration is that the lifting air in a thermal may be spinning due to the action of the inrushing air at lift-off, as mentioned earlier. If you circle in the opposite direction of the rotating thermal, you will achieve a given diameter circle with less bank and thus, a better sink rate. Sailplane pilots disregard this matter, since any significant rotation of a thermal is stopped by the time it climbs to an altitude useful for thermaling in such large craft. However, hang glider pilots often thermal near the ground, so it is useful to investigate thermal rotation.

Your best bet is to try circling both ways (clockwise and counterclockwise) in a thermal large enough to warrant changing direction, to see what provides the best rate of climb. On the average, if thermals are rotating, they probably turn clockwise most often in the Northern Hemisphere in harmony with the Coriolis force. However, be aware that just as dust devils can rotate both ways, so can a thermal. Much more investigation needs to be performed on this matter. A hang glider is an ideal thermal scouting device. Eventually, we will acquire considerable knowledge of thermal behavior heretofore unknown.

SOURCES OF VARIOMETER ERROR

How accurate are the varios used for hang gliding? As we shall see, there are several sources of error in a vario's readout. Once we understand these errors, they will not reduce the effectiveness of our varios in detecting thermals and joining the core.

One source of error is temperature and humidity changes on different days and at different altitudes. We all know that air density changes with temperature and humidity. When the air is less dense, a given vertical velocity will produce less drop in pressure, so less air will flow in and out of the flask, resulting in a low reading. For this reason, most varios are temperature compensated.

A similar type of error not compensated for in variometers employing air flow sensing, is that of pressure changes with altitude. In a manner similar to the previous error, these variometers will read low at any altitude above that for which they were originally calibrated. An error of about 3% per thousand feet is exhibited by all but aneroid type various due to altitude factors. For example, if you are 6,000 feet above the calibrated level of your vario, it will read too low by almost 20%.

The last source of error caused by the atmosphere is due to the movement of high and low pressure systems. When a widespread low pressure area moves in, our varios read lower than they should. All of these density errors are described by the following formula: $V_a = V_i \ (d_c/d_a)$, where V_a = actual vertical velocity; V_i = indicated vertical velocity; d_c = density of the air at which the vario was calibrated; and d_a = actual density of the air.

In a hang glider, it is not too important to compensate for these errors since values of lift will still register greater or lesser, according to their relative strength. In general, a hang glider must make efficient use of the lift in a small area and not be too worried about shooting out a mile or so to look for better lift, a technique that requires more accurate knowledge of the absolute vertical velocity of the air.

An internal source of error in a variometer is that of delay, both in initiation and extinction of the signal when vertical motion starts or stops. This is due to inherent delays in the electronic circuitry as well as gradual cooling and heating of the flask at different altitudes. You can note the delay in your variometer by feeling a surge of lift or sink on a moderate thermal day, then waiting for the audio or visual response. Typical varios experience a delay from fractions of a second to over several seconds. With practice you can compensate for this.

The variation of flask temperature is a matter more difficult to deal with since ambient temperature, rate and duration of climb is involved. However, in general, we should understand that after we have been climbing or sinking for some time, our vario will continue to indicate lift or sink for a period (possibly over 20 seconds after long climbs) even after we have stopped our rise or fall. This error is worse for rapid climbs and varies greatly with variometer design.

The final problem we should be aware of when using a vario, is that of pilot-induced changes in vertical velocity, or "stick thermals." When you are flying in still air and suddenly pull into a dive, or push out to climb when flying fast, a fall or rise will naturally register on your vario. This is proper, since you *are* changing your vertical velocity (see Figure 64). However, when thermaling, the vario will not distinguish these stick thermals from the real thing. Thus, total-energy variometers were developed to detect airspeed as well as vertical velocity and thereby correct for changes in vertical velocity due to nosing the craft up or down. Total-energy variometers are commonly used in sailplanes. Hang glider pilots, with their bodies in the airstream, should develop the ability to detect airspeed changes and thus stick thermals through practice. Of course, practicing efficient and intuitive control is half the fun of thermal flying.

In passing, we should mention the netto variometer. This device automatically compensates for the sink rate of the aircraft at all speeds, thus giving the vertical velocity of the airmass not the aircraft. This is very useful when following speed-to-fly techniques (see Chapter III).

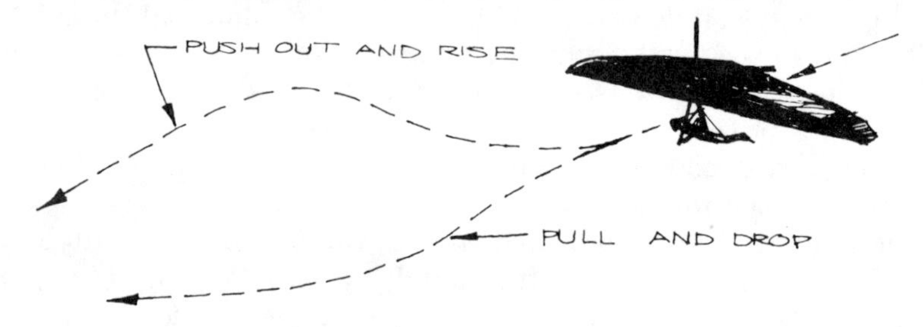

Figure 64 · Stick Thermals

USING YOUR VARIO

Let's assume you've just purchased a shiny new ultrasensitive, quadruple range, audio-visual, fur-lined stereo vario with the optional woofer and tweeter speakers. Now, how do you use it?

First, you must mount it on your glider in an easy to see and reachable location. Hose clamps holding the vario bracket to the control bar down tube is the most expedient method. However, mounting in this manner tends to result in a turning direction preference since it is much easier to observe the vario when turning to the side it is mounted on. A solution for prone pilots is to put the vario at the end of a bracket extending forward and to the center of the control bar. Be sure to keep it within reach so you can change ranges, adjust the audio or turn it on or off in flight.

Once you are ready to fly with your vario in its chosen place, turn it on a couple of minutes before your final pre-launch check to let it warm up. Once the readout has stabilized, adjust the vario to indicate zero lift. Check this several times; remember, you cannot zero-adjust your vario in flight with any degree of accuracy. (Most pilots prefer to set the readout slightly below zero so that they are not bothered with extraneous, unworkable bits of lift.)

Now, have a good takeoff and explore the sky. As you fly along, glance at your vario to get a feeling for your sink rate in level flight out of lift or sink. If you feel any lift or sink, watch to see how your vario responds. See if you can relate the strength of any lift or sink to the vario's readout. Do you notice how sometimes a sudden reduction in your rate of sink feels like lift? A glance at your vario will let you know when you encounter this "fool's lift."

If you run into a thermal, fly straight through it and count the seconds that you remain in the lift. This will give you a good idea of the extent of this particular lift patch. If you are flying 20 mph, you are moving almost 30 feet per second. Remember, you'll need a "three second thermal" to allow you to circle in the lift at a reasonable bank angle. Only the strongest thermals will allow you to really roll into a tight circle without decreasing your climb rate.

If you have plenty of clearance from the terrain, turn a 180 and see if you can enter the thermal again. This time, judge when you are 2/3 of the way across by counting seconds, then begin a 360 (in the same direction you turned the 180). As you continue circling, widen or tighten your turn and note if your climb rate changes. In this manner, you can maximize your climb. Also, try changing your bank angle during a given portion of the 360 so that you lengthen only one portion of the circle. This action will translate you in the direction of the lengthened arc. Again watch your vario for signs of improvement or loss.

Of course, it's very rare to find an accommodating thermal that will let you do so much experimenting in one flight. However, using your vario as a three dimensional mapping device will teach you to judge the strength, size and composition of different thermals in a surprisingly few number of flights.

Once you have learned a bit about thermal anatomy through exploration, you can begin to rely on a specific technique to help you find the cores or areas of best lift quickly and efficiently. There are several such techniques in practice, but the following method combines the best attributes of the others.

Like a moth around a light bulb you want to avoid areas of sink and spend as much time as possible near the hot thermal core. To do this, simply *reduce your bank angle when lift is increasing, and steepen your turn when lift is decreasing*. The angle of bank should vary from zero to 60°, being most often 20° to 30°, depending on the size and strength of the thermals. Without a vario, this may be hard to follow in weak conditions.

Let's look at a hypothetical thermal and see how this technique works. In Figure 65 we see a nice fat thermal just waiting to offer a ride. Assume we are blundering along through the sky until we encounter lift at A. It increases, so we continue flying straight until our vario winds down at B. We make a left turn (the wrong way) and encounter sink, so we steepen our turn at C, then flatten it again when lift increases at D. We continue on through the center of the thermal and again turn sharper at E when the lift diminishes, continuing around to F where we open up the turn at the sign of better lift. At G the lift starts lessening so we again bank steeper, then continue around in the same radius since we are now centered in the core and the lift is fairly constant. We circle upward at H with our vario broadcasting our luck.

Notice that the pilot in our illustration turns only to the left. In reality, an experienced thermal flyer can pick up subtle clues that help him turn toward the core more readily. For example, the stretch between A and B as well as D and E would most likely tend to roll a glider to the left since stronger lift is on the right. A sensitive pilot would turn right when the lift began to decrease during these portions of the flight path.

The majority of thermals have several cores. Use this technique to center you in the best one you encounter. Don't be afraid to alter your bank and turn direction often. Watch the example of the hawks and vultures in this matter.

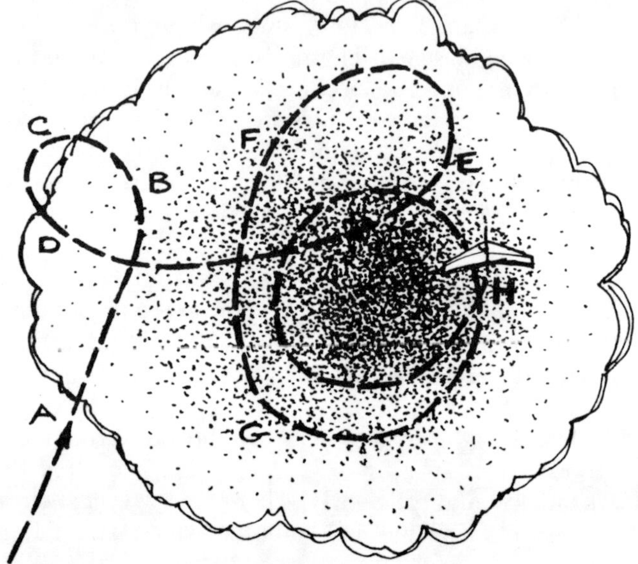

Figure 65 - Locating the Core

SPECIAL CONDITIONS

When wind is present, thermals drift and tilt. To remain within a thermal, a pilot must drift along with the thermal as he circles. If we are within the main body of the thermal, performing even banked 360's will provide the proper drift since the wind will push us along with the thermal. However, the situation is different in a slanted column thermal.

In Figure 66, we see a pilot exploiting the lift in a long, slanted column. If he continued to perform regular, continuous 360's, he would fall out below the column as shown at A. This is because his climb rate is always less than that of the rising air and thus, his path is not as steep. The remedy for such a fate is to flatten the upwind portion of the turn thereby repositioning the circular path into the thermal column by lengthening the upwind leg. Of course, the signal of your vario will let you know when this situation occurs, and following the technique of changing bank angle with varying lift will keep you centered in the column.

Another special situation occurs near a ridge in windy conditions. It has been observed by many pilots (myself included) that when circling in a thermal in these conditions, the upwind leg of the turn produces markedly better lift than the downwind leg. This can only be explained by the existence of a gradient—that is, increasing lift on the upwind leg and decreasing lift on the downwind portion. One theory on this matter is that the difference is produced by the tilting of the thermal caused by the wind gradient. This has

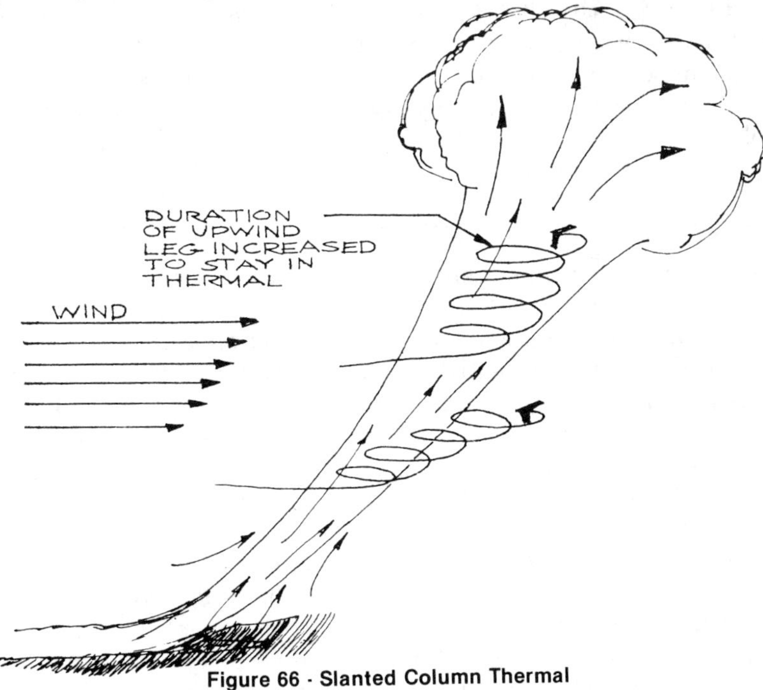

Figure 66 · Slanted Column Thermal

two effects: first, the air enters the thermal at an oblique angle, and secondly, the lift is stronger away from the ridge. Thus as shown in Figure 67, a pilot turning on the downwind leg at A encounters diminishing lift. When he turns upwind at B he encounters suddenly increasing lift which then results in greater climb in the upwind leg.

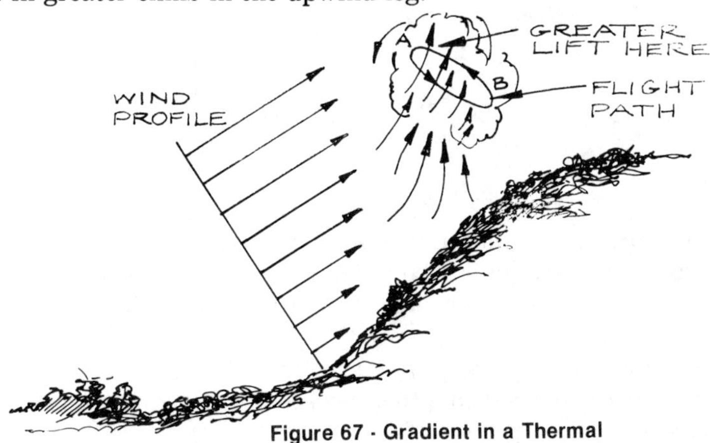

Figure 67 · Gradient in a Thermal

As yet, there are many aspects of flying near the ground that still need investigating. A vario is an invaluable tool for checking out micrometeorological phenomena. In everyday thermal flying, a vario is most useful at high altitudes and in very light conditions. I thermaled extensively for three years before I bought a vario. When I did, I found my climbing ability was improved significantly when I was away from visual cues such as the terrain or other gliders. I often turn my vario off to practice flying by sense of feel, sight, sound and smell. However, when I'm trying to eke out the last bit of lift in any airmass, my vario is by my side warbling away. Remember, the mark of a good pilot is versatility. Learn to sniff out the lift in all conditions—with and without a vario.

CROSS COUNTRY DOWN A RIDGE

Paralleling a ridge or mountain chain is the way most pilots begin their cross country experience. When flying along a ridge, lift is generally dependable so it is desirable to fly as fast as possible to make time. One method I worked out in the early standard days was to fly a bit in front of the ridge to remain at lower altitudes, thus encountering less wind which in turn requires less of a crab angle, thereby allowing faster progress along the ridge. Of course, at times it is necessary to slow up, move in to the ridge and work thermals to cross gaps, broken stretches or areas where the ridge turns away from the wind.

A hypothetical flight along an imaginary ridge is shown in Figure 68. Here, our knowledgeable pilot starts on the right, well away from the ridge in order to make better time. When the pilot reaches point A where the ridge angles back, he moves to the best lift area above the ridge top and speeds up to traverse the area of reduced lift as quickly as possible. Once the area of better lift is achieved (B), the pilot resumes his or her normal progress.

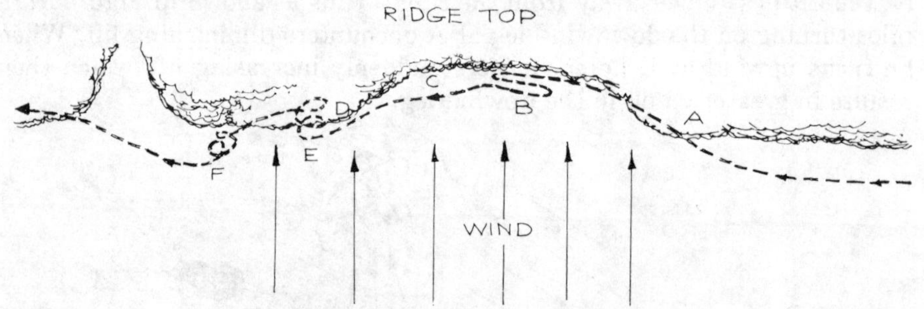

Figure 68 · Ridge Soaring Technique

However, the presence of another change in the ridge direction requires a revision of tactics. The pilot will be flying into a bit of a headwind as well as reduced lift from C to D, so working lift in the vicinity of B and possibly flying away from the mountain in zero sink to reduce the headwind component is the best tactic. In both cases where the mountain slants away from the wind, lift is reduced so increasing flying speed is in order as in normal speed-to-fly techniques (see Chapter III).

The headwind run from C to D calls for the greatest increase in airspeed. Of course, if the entire ridge is slanted to the wind, it may be necessary to fly near minimum sink speed to maximize the lift. Speed-to-fly techniques only apply when the areas of lift are quite variable.

When thermals are encountered in ridge soaring conditions, it is best to only stay in them for a few turns to avoid wasting time and also losing all the altitude you gained (and then some) in the thermal by trying to get back to the front of the ridge in sink and a headwind. It is better to ride the thermal back only a short distance, then exit from the side, angling to the front of the ridge as shown in E.

When a gap is encountered, it is best to thermal up but work in front of the mountain as much as possible, so that when the run across the gap is attempted, the flight path will be somewhat downwind (as shown at F). Pulling on a little extra speed is in order here. The wind can escape through a gap like a safety valve, providing little lift and lots of headwind, so be sure to allow plenty of extra altitude.

Flying along the formidable mountain chains in the west requires a different approach. For example, the great height of the White Mountains that border the Owens Valley create an abundance of large, powerful thermals, while the high pressure dominated weather patterns keep the winds light. Thus, while it is still necessary to follow the lay of the mountains to remain in the area of abundant thermal generation, the actual utilization of lift is as if the pilot were flying free from terrain effects. The techniques of this type of flying are discussed in the next section.

The key to successful cross-country flying along a ridge is knowing when to work lift, when to leave thermals to continue on, when to maximize groundspeed and how to cross non-productive portions of the ridge. When thermals are present in conjunction with ridge lift, large areas of sink can appear as readily as improved lift. Of course, a day when you get high quickly only to be let down rapidly is not the best for tallying up the mileage. A certain amount of dependable altitude (due to ridge lift) is very useful for crossing the difficult areas.

CROSS COUNTRY OVER THE TOP

In many parts of the country, the only way for a pilot to achieve a long distance flight is to get high, then turn downwind, since many sites consist of isolated hills or mountains. There are, of course, certain techniques and cautions that should be observed when going "over the top."

The perfect day for leaving a mountain on a downwind trek will exhibit abundant, strong thermals and a moderate wind (perhaps 15 mph at launch). These conditions will allow a pilot to climb quite high without drifting too far behind takeoff before a final thermal is boarded for the ride up and away.

There are several points to remember: It is dangerous to drift behind the front of a ridge or mountain unless you are maintaining at least a two to one glide path with this front portion. The loss of a thermal and subsequent sink can drop you in the rough on top of the mountain, or put you in air that will slap you around if you settle down close behind the mountain (see Figure 69).

The second point to remember is: never fly over the back of a mountain of any significant size with less than 1,000 feet clearance above the top. When you do decide to go for it, be sure to head downwind without hesitation to avoid the leeside turbulence (swirling air formed behind the mountain). Finally, be sure to go over the top only in thermal conditions. If you are getting high only in ridge lift or wave lift, chances are there will be powerful rotors downwind from the mountain. In the latter case, these rotors (standing eddies) may be several miles behind the mountain. Make no mistake about it, pilots have been injured or killed by failing to heed these commonsense rules.

Once you have acquired all the altitude you can get in front of the ridge or mountain, it's time to select the best thermal you can find and follow it as far as possible upwards and backwards. Don't be hasty. Shop around and look for a thermal with a good deal of workable lift. Once you have made your choice, use all your well-practiced thermaling skills to remain in the core and rise quickly.

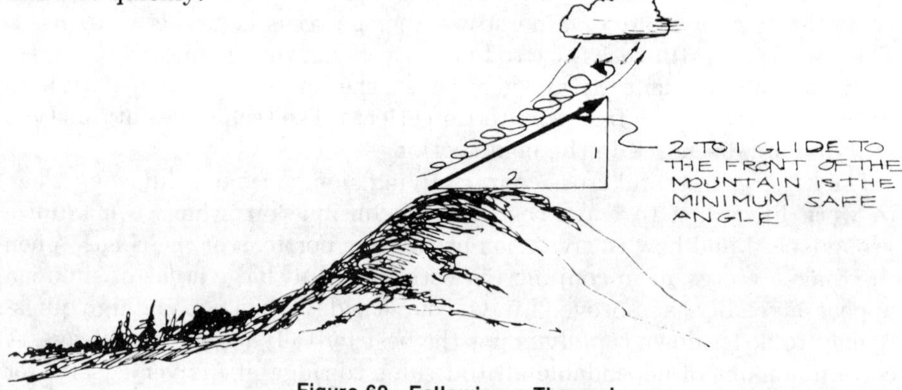

Figure 69 · Following a Thermal

Of course, you will be drifting downwind – behind the mountain – but be careful to avoid falling out below a tilted thermal. Most thermals above a ridge are columnar and tilted, so a little extra upwind flying is in order.

Once your breakaway thermal has died, or diminished greatly, it's time to move on. Your flight path should aim directly downwind. This is for two reasons. First, the downwind direction will carry you further since a tailwind increases your glide slope with respect to the ground. Secondly, if your first thermal is part of a cloudstreet, you will stay in the street by flying downwind.

Cloudstreets occur quite often on thermal-producing days. Of course, if the thermals are ending in cumulus clouds, it will be easy to detect streets. However, when thermals are dry ("blue thermals"), streets may form just as readily ("blue streets"), so a downwind run is optimum if aspects of the terrain do not invite an alteration of course.

When encountering free thermals or lift in streets, it is best to climb as high as possible before setting out for the next lift area. Hang gliders are not yet so efficient that they can give up diminishing lift to speed to the next thermal as is common practice when flying sailplanes. This rule should be modified somewhat in areas where lift extends very high (the West) so that the dangers of hypoxia are not encountered. In the East, it is a rare day when cloudbase reaches even 12,000 feet ASL, so hypoxia is not a problem.

Figure 70 illustrates an ideal flight along a cloudstreet. Isolated thermals require the same technique, although the spacing of the thermals is much greater, so the time spent climbing will be greater at A and B. At point C, the pilot encounters widespread lift, so straight-ahead flight is expedient. The important policy to adhere to when cross-country flying in thermals is to use speed-to-fly techniques. This means you speed up in sink and slow down in lift, an amount dependent on your glider's polar (performance graph). We are interested in using lift in the most efficient manner, more than maximizing speed since we need all the altitude we can get over open country (of course, it is nice to travel as quickly as possible if it is late afternoon and the thermals are dying). Thus, in the free sky, we ignore the effects of horizontal wind (headwind or tailwind) and apply speed-to-fly principles only to the vertical components encountered.

Figure 70 · Flying Along a Cloud Street

The thing to remember is that thermals are moving with the wind so we must speed through the sink between the thermals, despite the fact that a tailwind would normally require slowing down to achieve the best distance over the ground.

Very often cloudstreets or isolated thermals stop in a general area known as a "blue hole." This can be caused by an intrusion of cold air or a wet surface (swamp, lake, etc.). It is usually advisable to detour around these areas. Of course, climbing as high as possible in the last visible thermal is most important when striking out across non-promising airspace (see point D in Figure 70).

If the street you are in terminates up ahead, but one to either side continues further, it may be wise to try to cross the area of sink between the streets. In general, streets tend to be spaced about 2½ times the height of the clouds. Thus, a 2.5 to 1 glide slope appears to be sufficient to reach the neighboring street. This is not quite right since it is desirable to reach the street high (at least half way between the surface and the clouds) and the general sink between the streets actually steepens the glide slope. Thus, better than a 10 to 1 glide ratio may be required to hop between streets.

Crossing the streets in a hang glider is thus a matter of chance. If landing areas are abundant, go ahead and try it. Take the shortest route possible to the best looking cloud and speed up through the sink. Once you reach the new street, fly along under it for the best chance of picking up the lift.

If you are on a final glide with no hope of finding lift, then the horizontal wind velocity should be taken into consideration – speed up in a headwind, slow down in a tailwind – to maximize distance over the ground.

LANDING OUT

One of the most important parts of cross-country flying is landing safely. Since you will be landing in unknown areas not previously scrutinized, it is necessary to learn to judge a landing field from the air. The important matters to discern are the wind direction, roughness of the field, the slope of the field and the presence of power lines. The wind direction on the ground can be foretold by watching smoke plumes, drifting dust, flags waving, trees and grass rippling, as well as wind lines on water (see Figure 71).

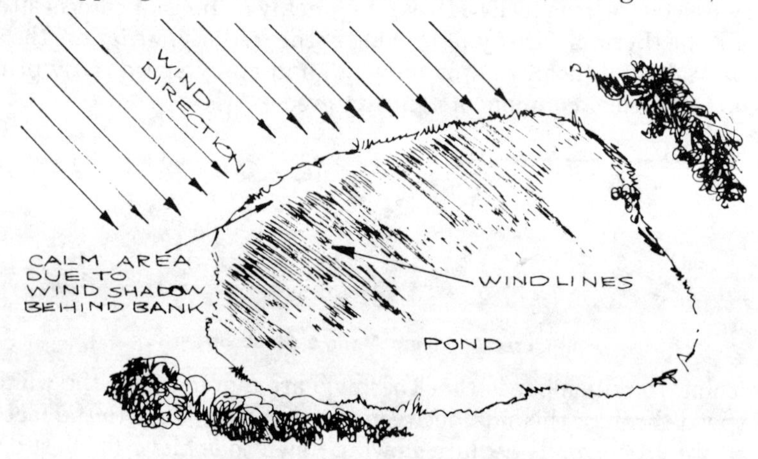

Figure 71 · Wind Lines on Water

The roughness of a field isn't too hard to determine from the air as long as you are aware that what appears to be bushes and ruts from 1,000 feet up may be small trees and ditches in actuality. The slope of a field may be indicated by erosion lines, cultivation markings (farmers normally plow perpendicular to the fall line or slope direction) and the presence of water courses (the ground slopes toward a stream).

Power lines are insidious. Often, a pole will be hidden in trees while the wire stretches across your landing field. To detect such atrocities, look for cuts in the trees as well as the presence of buildings. One can generaly assume that every building as well as road harbors a nearby power line. Try to trace the path of these lines long before you get too low to change your choice of fields. Remember, landing out (away from home base) can be complicated, so practice reading terrain and conditions from the air on every flight you take. Figure 72 illustrates some of the things to look for.

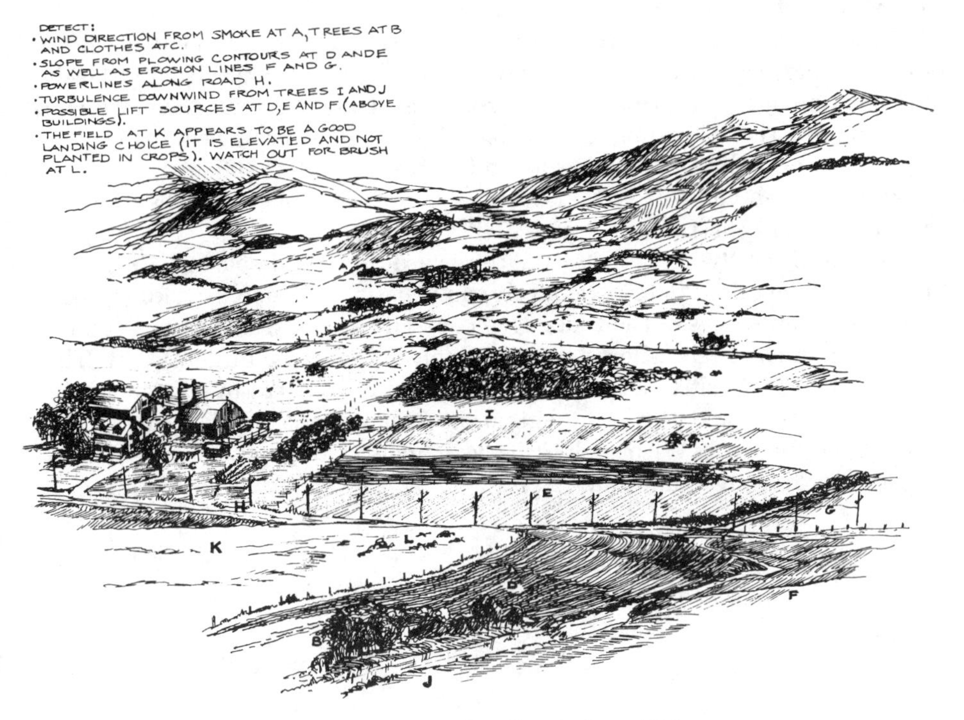

Figure 72 · Reading Terrain from Aloft

FURTHER DANGERS

Besides the cautions expressed above, it's important to be aware of a few other dangers associated with cross-country thermal flying. One danger is the possibility of encountering severe thermal-induced turbulence. The best way to minimize this danger is to not fly in strong winds. If the wind is strong, thermals are usually torn apart and not workable anyway. If the thermals themselves are exceptionally strong, be prepared to go over the falls a time or two. This disconcerting experience occurs when flying on the border of a rolling thermal. With practice, a pilot can learn to predict the presence of the "falls" by noting the changing lift in the thermal. It is best to hold a little speed when expecting such a pitch change. Of course, a parachute is mandatory operating equipment in any thermal condition.

Another precaution when flying cross-country is the avoidance of air traffic. A hang glider would fare little better than a June bug on a windshield in an encounter with a jumbo jet. Smaller aircraft pose even more of a problem since they are more likely to be encountered at altitudes reached by hang gliders. To reduce the chance of such an unpleasant confrontation, avoid flying near Victor airways and VOR stations. These items are part of the navigation system used by general aviation pilots. Victor airways are the light blue lines connecting the VOR stations on sectional maps. Learn their location for your area. Note that a pilot may be flying a couple of miles or so to one side of the airway.

If you must cross an area of traffic, be constantly alert for airplanes at all levels in all directions. Know the approved flight heading at different levels and set your altimeter to register absolute altitude above sea level, so you too can obey these headings. On a clear day (VFR) aircraft heading east of the north/south line should be at odd thousands plus 500 feet. Aircraft heading west should be flying at even thousands plus 500 feet. The levels in between are for instrument flight.

Cross-country flying is the ultimate reward of skillful soaring. Ridge lift alone just won't do. Pilots at all levels can benefit from increased knowledge of the ways and wiles of thermals. Even a beginner can start thinking about the shape of thermals when she/he flies through an area of gentle lift. The key to efficient thermal soaring is a lot of practice to perform efficient turns of varying bank and a good imagination to help perceive the path of the elusive thermal core. With such skills we may all find our own magic streets to carry us for miles and miles...

CHAPTER VI

DESIGN CONCEPTS

A hang glider is unique among aircraft. Not only is it ultra-light for portability, but weight shift control, flexible airfoils, variable washout and billow shift are standard hang glider features that are unknown to other aircraft. The designer of hang gliders is challenged to understand the intricacies of hang glider aerodynamics. Much of the information cannot be found in textbooks, for we are dealing with a new breed of aircraft. The hang glider pilot is also challenged to learn to use the special controls of his craft with the utmost skill to maximize flying efficiency. This chapter is devoted to understanding how our gliders work. This understanding is a prerequisite to becoming a knowledgeable, expert pilot.

We will investigate four areas of hang glider design. These are: stability, handling, performance and structure. In truth, these four areas of concern are intricately connected; a designer has to compromise one to enhance the other. Let's see how this trade-off comes about in state-of-the-art gliders.

STABILITY

Unfortunately, stability and handling are at opposite ends of the pole. Too much stability results in slow, heavy handling, while a great handling ship may be somewhat unstable. The trick is to tread the thin line between good handling and adequate stability when designing and tuning a hang glider.

Pitch stability refers to the tendency of the glider to return to level flight when its angle of attack is increased or decreased by an external force. For instance, a stable glider will want to pull its nose up if a thermal knocks it into a dive; it will want to nose down if a thermal lifts the nose. The stronger the forces the glider exerts to return to normal flight, the more stable it is said to be.

Pitch stability in a hang glider can be achieved by developing a stable root section (center of the glider), or using the tip area to control pitching moments. Look at Figure 73. Here we see a common airfoil shape and the upward force it develops at different angles of attack. Unfortunately, at low angles of attack the airfoil wants to dive more since the lifting force moves behind the center of gravity (C.G.). At high angles of attack, the airfoil wants to nose up more since the lifting force moves ahead of the C.G. Thus, we conclude that such an airfoil is unstable.

If we use a shape like the airfoil in the figure for the center section of our glider, then we need to make some other arrangement for pitch stability. An airplane uses its tail to insure pitch stability. Our two wing tips trailing behind the center of mass of the glider serve very nicely as a tail. Certain designs employ truncated tips or swivel tips that hold the sail at a lower

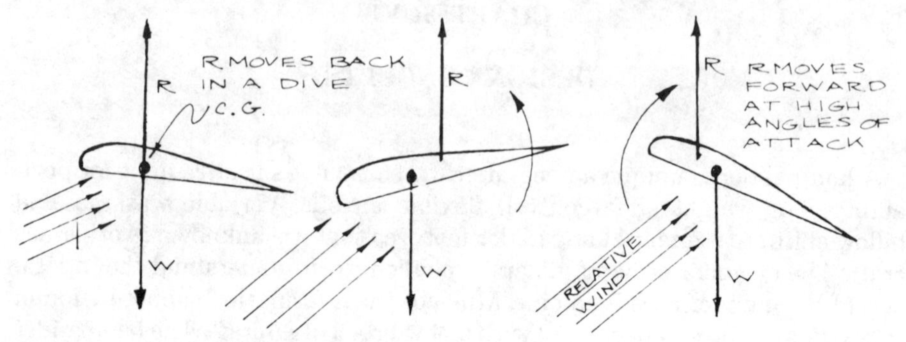

Figure 73 · Pitch Stability

angle of attack at the tips than at the root. This serves to prevent dives in the following manner: at normal flying speeds, lift is developed along the wing as shown in Figure 74(a). As the pilot speeds up (lowers his angle of attack), the lifting force moves back a bit at each section, but lift is greatly reduced at the tips since they are held at even a lower angle of attack than the root section. The net effect is a resultant upward force that actually moves ahead of the C.G. as in 74(b), instead of behind. Consequently, the glider wants to nose up out of the dive.

In a high angle of attack situation, the reverse process takes place. The tips work harder and tend to pull the rear of the glider up and thus lower the angle of attack. Actually, a glider without any special tip arrangement will work in the same way to produce pitch stability. However, a problem exists

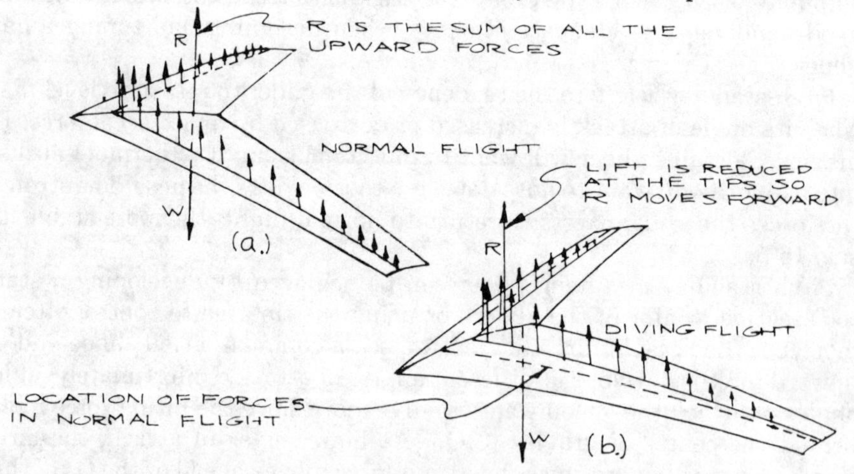

Figure 74 · Glider Stability

at extremely low angles of attack (in a steep dive). In this case, the pilot may be unweighted so that the coupling between the upward force and his weight doesn't create a positive pitching moment (nose up force). The entire sail may be flagging and developing very little lift. Only a special arrangement such as fixed washout (truncated tips), defined tips (see Figure 2) or a reflex bridle system (a number of lines from the top of the kingpost to the rear of the inboard batterns) can pull a glider out of a steep dive by itself. You can stand at the nose of a glider with such devices and see how the tips and rear of the sail present their top surfaces at low angles of attack. This concept is explained in more detail in Chapter VI of *Hang Gliding Flying Skills*.

Certain airfoils are stable by themselves. These are reflexed airfoils as depicted in Figure 75. If a reflexed airfoil is used in the root section, a designer can achieve pitch stability without setting his fixed washout at the tips too high. This will allow the glider to develop better lift at higher speeds. This, of course, means good performance for a wider speed range. The problem is, however, a reflexed airfoil suffers somewhat in low speed performance. So we come to the designer's dilemma: how much to trade off root performance for tip performance in the quest for a necessarily pitch stable glider. Currently, there are designs available representing one extreme to the other.

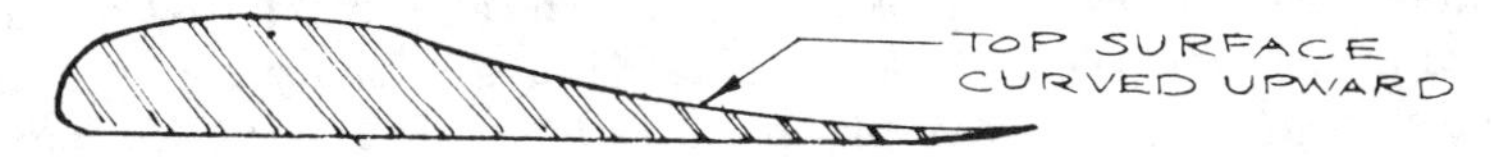

Figure 75 · Reflexed Airfoil

HANDLING

A glider must be easy to control to be a fun flying glider. This means pitch and roll changes are fairly light pressured and uncontrollable yawing does not take place. Pitch control usually doesn't present a problem with modern gliders. Wider nose angles (less sweep angles) as seen on these gliders mean less area behind and in front of the pilot (see Figure 76). The result is less damping in pitch which means lighter control pressure. Of course, as less sweep is employed, the tips are less effective in doing their pitch stability duty – another design trade-off.

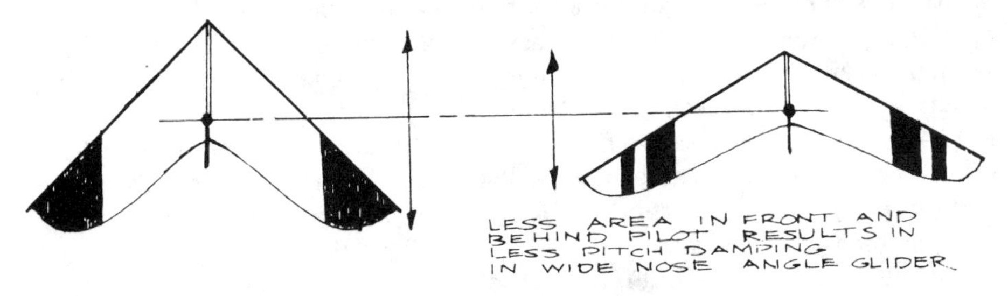

Figure 76 · Pitch Damping

Damping is both a friend and a foe. Whereas stability is a force returning a glider to equilibrium, damping acts on a glider only when it is rolling, yawing or pitching. For instance, the roll rate of a glider is slowed or "damped" in two ways: the inertia of the glider's mass resists change and the sail drags against the air as one wing moves down and the other up. In this case, damping is a foe. However, some damping is necessary to keep a glider from oscillating once it is disturbed from straight and level flight.

As a rule, designers are constantly trying to remove damping in roll–there always seems to be an excess. Wider wingspans and heavier gliders add to the problem. Some methods for reducing roll damping are lightening the tips and introducing flexible tips. Flexible tips act like a weather vane and allow the wing to move up or down easier in a roll. In turbulence they actually have a smoothing effect since they relieve the load when a gust hits.

Like too much damping, too much stability in roll can make a glider slow or difficult to turn. Roll stability is the tendency for the glider to keep its wings level. *Too much* roll stability results in poor handling since the glider resists banking of the wings when the pilot tries to turn. *Too little* roll stability results in spiral instability–the glider wants to roll of its own accord and enters a steeper and steeper spiral when it is banked.

To understand how roll stability and handling relate to design factors in our gliders, we should first look at how a turn takes place. In Chapter II, we saw the important role that adverse yaw plays in the turning process of a weight-shift glider. For example, a glider entering a left turn yaws to the right briefly while it is rolling left, then starts yawing left. The brief adverse yaw to the right represents a left slip (turn back to Figure 19 and 22 to see why). When a glider is in a left slip, it appears to the wind striking the wings as shown in Figure 77. Three types of wings are shown. The first is a wing with dihedral, the second is a wing with anhedral and the third is a wing very similar to a hang glider sail form. Note that the hang glider has a dihedral shape in the center (root) section, and an anhedral shape in the outer (tip) sections.

Looking at the dihedral wing, we see that in a left slip the left wing is at a higher angle of attack (presents more surface to the airflow) than the right wing. Consequently, the left wing will lift more than the right wing and work to prevent a roll to the left. This wing shape has good stability, but is not too desirable for weight-shift control. As an illustration, make a model of a flying wing out of paper or styrofoam, shape it like a hang glider without a tail and add dihedral in the wings. Once you get the model flying straight, add a small weight to the left wing. Would you expect it to turn left? You may be surprised to find it turns right, due to adverse yaw and the effect of dihedral as explained above. The only way to get a dihedral wing to turn properly is to add a rudder (the solution for airplanes) or tip dragging devices (for flying wings).

For the anhedral wing in Figure 77, the left slip lowers the angle of attack on the left wing and raises it on the right wing. This results in the right wing lifting more than the left, which helps the glider roll to the left when the pilot shifts his weight to the left. Thus, an anhedral shape promotes quick, light roll control. However, a strictly anhedral wing is usually spirally instable.

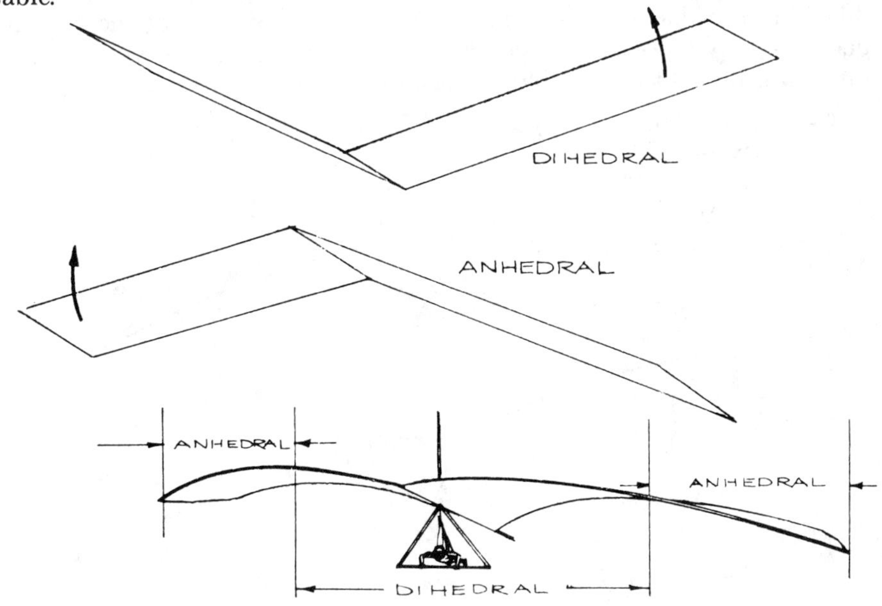

Figure 77 · Effects of Anhedral and Dihedral

In a hang glider, the sail shape produces a stable dihedral midsection with anhedral tips that aid the roll control. In Figure 77 we can see that the right tip is at a much higher angle of attack than the left tip. This helps the pilot roll left. Note how bowing the leading edges adds to the anhedral effect of the tips. By varying the anhedral dihedral balance of a sail, the designer can, to a great extent, control the handling characteristics of a glider. If a glider is "dihedrally dominated" it may be difficult to turn using weight shift.

An integral part of a glider's turning ability is the amount of sweep in the wing (less sweep is the same as a wider nose angle). The less sweep a glider has, the less yaw stability it has. Too little sweep can lead to adverse yaw problems as show in Figure 78. Here we see a glider with a 180 ° nose angle and one with a 120 ° nose angle approaching in a slight left slip caused by the pilot initiating a left turn by shifting his weight. In the unswept wing, the drag distribution is unfavorable – there is more drag area to the right of the pilot than to the left. Since gravity pulling the pilot's body is the main source of thrust, this glider would continue to yaw adversely to the right. The glider with a smaller nose angle has a favorable drag distribution. In this case, the adverse yaw to the right is quickly changed to a left yaw which helps the roll and produces a coordinated left turn.

Too much sweep can present problems also. At a certain point, increasing the sweep will have the same effect as dihedral in over-stabilizing a wing. In addition, the more swept back a wing is, the harder the required push out in a turn, the lower the performance in general and the more susceptible the glider is to tip stalls. The designer must carefully form the anhedral/-dihedral sail balance for the amount of sweep he chooses (and vice-versa) to get a properly yaw-roll coupled glider. If he does not, pilots will quickly let him know his glider turns like a truck or handles "squirrely."

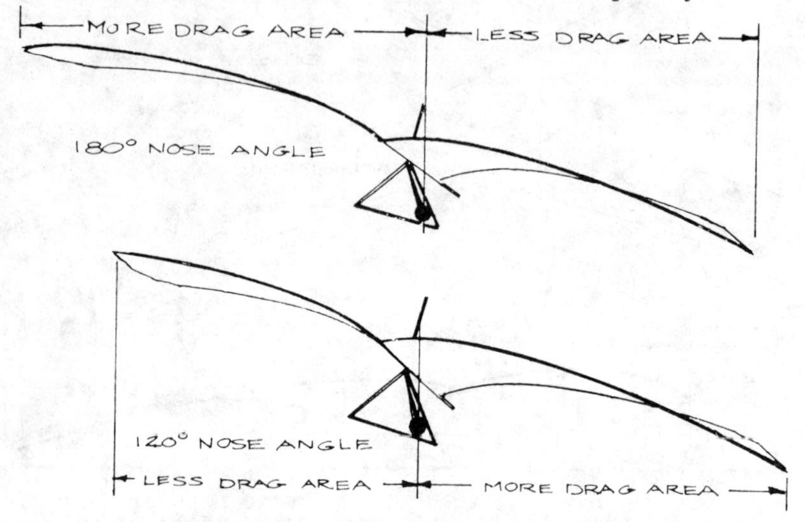

Figure 78 · Sweep and Drag Distribution

Of course, the designer can rely on other tricks to get an easy turning glider. These are flexible tips, floating crossbar and billow shift. As previously mentioned, flexible tips reduce roll damping and help the sail conform to the necessary turn helix. A slower turn can be made with flexible tips since the glider can be pushed to a higher angle of attack. A slower turn results in a smaller turn radius for a given angle of bank.

Billow shift causes an unequal lift distribution on the wings in a turn, which greatly aids roll initiation. This is explained in detail in Chapter II. Billow shift is provided for with stand-up keel pockets. Raised keel pockets allow the sail to move from side to side at the keel. A floating cross bar allows the keel to shift from side to side in flight. When a pilot shifts his weight to the left, for example, the pull of the hang strap moves the keel to the left of the centerline. This movement results in lighter bar pressures (in roll) since a pilot has to raise himself less for a given sideways displacement.

Besides creating a glider that rolls easily, a designer must also concern himself with turn roll-out, tip stalling and landing characteristics. In a turn, the inside tip is at a much higher angle of attack than the outside tip. A designer can take advantage of this fact by introducing the proper shape camber in the tip battens. Varying the camber (and thus the airfoil shape) varies the lift produced at different angles of attack. Consequently, a glider can be made to roll out of a turn or ideally have neutral roll stability by adjusting the tip camber.

Tip stalling can also be controlled by adding camber to the tips. This allows the angle of attack of the tip to reach a higher value before a stall occurs. The high point of the wing's airfoil should move rearward and the percent camber of the chord should increase toward the tips for maximum benefit. Other ways to reduce tip stalling is to employ a wider nose angle (less sweep) and a higher taper ratio. Taper ratio is defined as the tip chord divided by the root chord. For a taper ratio of one, the tip is the same size as the root. A lower taper ratio relates to a pointed or small tip. Tip stalling occurs in part because span-wise flow increases the loading at the tips. All the above remedies help reduce this effect.

Landings are made easier when tip stalling is reduced. Flexible tips also help since they allow the tips to wash out and the glider parachutes in without stalling a wing. Quick turning ability is also an asset in a landing situation so that a pilot can make last minute maneuvers in tight areas. The handling of a glider is obviously very important for safety reasons both during landings and in flight. A designer must spend as much time working on control problems as he does on the glider's all important performance.

PERFORMANCE

Public pressure demands more and more performance from hang gliders. This demand usually means better glide ratios and lower sink rates. Over the years, designers have increased glide ratios by incorporating higher aspect ratios, wider spans, wider nose angles, tighter sails and battens.

Aspect ratio is a measure of how long and thin a wing is when viewed from the top. The higher the aspect ratio, the thinner the wing is. Higher aspect ratio wings produce better glide ratios (and sink rates) by decreasing the tip losses. As a wing moves through the air, spanwise flow occurs along the lower surface since the air tries to relieve the pressure difference between the top and the bottom of the wing by flowing around the tip. This results in the creation of wing tip vortices and a substantial loss in efficiency. Increasing the aspect ratio reduces this loss by creating a lower pressure difference between the top and bottom of the wing at the tip (the spanwise loading is less) and thereby reducing tip vortices.

As aspect ratios increased over the years so did performance until wider spans presented roll problems. The use of billow shift reduced the roll problem so that aspect ratio again increased to the present values of over six or seven. Increased efficiency allowed sail areas to be reduced from 230 square feet to around 160 sq. ft. for the same weight pilot.

The upper limit to aspect ratio is not necessarily handling, but parasitic drag and washout control. Increased spans and increased speeds take their toll by creating more glide-deteriorating drag. A thinner wing requires more sail tension in order to prevent excessive tip washout. Until streamlined pilots and better tips are developed, hang gliders will not begin to reach the 20 to 1 glide ratios of basic sailplanes.

The other most important reason for the gain in performance over earlier gliders is the use of tighter sails with battens. Tighter sails decreases the washout. Washout in a wing is a progressively lower angle of attack towards the tip. Washout reduces efficiency since only a small portion of the wing can be at the best angle of attack at one time. By tightening the sail on the frame, the designer can get the entire wing flying close to the same angle of attack (see Figure 79).

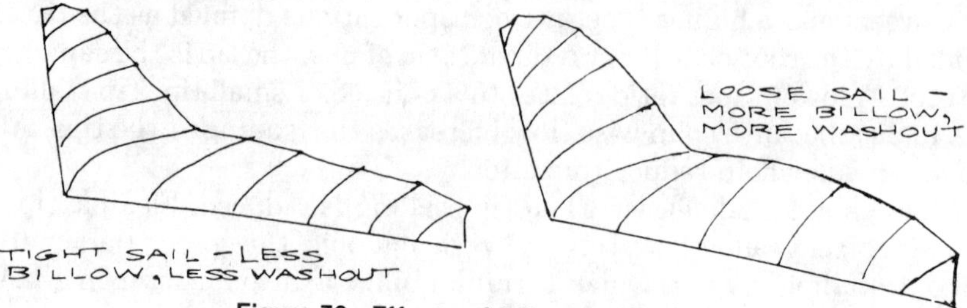

Figure 79 - Effects of Billow on Washout

The tighter the sail, the greater became the wing stalling problem (the tips no longer washed out). The solution was to add battens and roach so that at high angles of attack the tip area floated up while the mid-span washout was kept to a minimum. Designers are still experimenting with ideal washout curves and tip designs. Hopefully they will continue to deliver better solutions to the performance problems.

Many design factors that improve glide ratio also improve a glider's sink rate. Besides increased aspect ratio, less sweep, and tigher sails, we can add cambered and double surfaced sails. Camber in a sail is an airfoil shaped curve which produces a greater pressure difference between the upper and lower surface. This results in a higher maximum lift co-efficient and ultimately a better minimum sink rate. Double surface sails allow an increase in the mean camber in a wing without an equal increase in drag at high speeds. Single surface sails enjoy good performance at a limited (low) speed. At higher speeds – when penetrating a wind for instance – the single surface glider will drop more rapidly than its double surface counterpart.

Of course, one of the most important factors determining sink rate is wing loading. The lighter the wing loading, the lower the minimum sink rate. The lower limit to wing loading is handling (the larger the glider, the slower it responds) and penetration ability. If a glider had great handling and high speed performance, you could fly a larger size and win on all accounts. It's nice to have a good sink rate so that you can catch a soaring flight on those light wind days.

STRUCTURE

The final design consideration may be the most important one. Structural integrity is necessary in all designs to carry a pilot safely through bone jarring turbulence and tight maneuvers. As spans increased and sails tightened, the loads on the leading edges and crossbars increased geometrically. Unfortunately, failure of these structural parts in flight occurred before extensive testing lead to the use of deflexors and stronger tubing. Deflexors are struts with cables that keep the leading edges from bending under load. The bending force is translated to compression in the leading edge, so strong tubing is still required. Currently, cantilever wings are being employed to eliminate deflexors and reduce drag. A cantilever wing is one supported by its own internal structure. This means thick, heavy leading edges. Again, the cost of performance is weight.

Crossbars have grown in size from 1½ inches to up to 2 inches. A look at the forces involved explain why. A standard glider of a few years ago with a 4° billow sail would only have a crossbar compression of 180 lbs. Today's gliders with only a fraction of a degree billow can have up to 500 lbs. crossbar compression (depending on wing loading). Clearly the designer cannot afford to skimp on crossbar selection. The only other potential structural weak point is the control bar uprights. These "down tubes" undergo quite a bit of in-flight compression, they must be straight at all times. With longer control bar uprights as used in current designs, most manufacturers have taken to adding an internal sleeve for the required strength.

It should go without saying that a crossbar or control bar should never be used in a damaged condition. Crossbars must be replaced if bent. Control bars may be straightened only if the bend is very slight (one tube diameter or less). Otherwise, replace bent control bars, for bending and straightening a tube weakens it and leaves it susceptible to corrosion by cracking the surface anodizing.

Newer designs with cantilever wings fly with a bow in the leading edge due to the pull of the sail. Consequently, a designer must cut the sail to form this curve. This, of course, is not an easy matter to do as it is difficult to guess the exact shape of the leading edge in flight. Trial and error, along with a good dose of experience is useful in this instance. Adding camber to the sail at the wing tips is another common trick. This is accomplished by "broadseaming," or pulling the sail together at the trialing edge when a tip panel is sewed to its neighbor. The result is a sail that won't lay flat on the floor since it takes the shape of an inverted saucer. Cambering the sail helps control tip washout and reduce tip flutter.

Of course the ultimate limiting factor in a design is weight. Often higher performance and better handling require tricks and techniques which in turn requires stronger airframes which finally ends up adding weight. Hopefully, new materials such as fiberglass, titanium and carbon-graphite with their superior strength to weight ratio will become economically feasible for use in hang gliders.

It should be obvious that a designer has a difficult job trying to decide what parameters to trade off for different benefits. Very often he makes an educated guess, then starts building, testing, cutting, trying, flying, scrapping and rebuilding. All too often he finds he can only please a small segment of the flying population. Instead of copying the design of the fine soaring birds with their perfectly engineered shape and feathers, a designer is forced to copy the bats with their membrane wing stretched with bone battens. The problem is, soaring bats are unheard of.

CHAPTER VII

FLYING EQUIPMENT

Just as important as a pilot's flying ability is the flying ability of his glider. A pilot flying an intermediate glider can only climb so high and glide so far in a given amount of lift. A better performing glider will certainly carry him higher and further. Years ago, the difference in performance between the latest model glider and its predecessor was dramatic. Not so today. The hottest new design on the market may exhibit only the slightest increase in performance and this may be at the expense of light weight and simplicity. In this chapter we will look at ways to determine which is the right glider for you.

Some pilots change gliders as often as a bird molts its feathers. This isn't necessarily beneficial as it takes a while for a pilot to know every little quirk and nuance of a glider's handling and performance. To help you maximize your current glider's flying abilities, at the end of this chapter we will discuss the latest trimming tehniques. First, let's review equipment needs other than the glider.

EMERGENCY PARACHUTES

Since 1977, more and more pilots fly with a back-up parachute system. This added safety factor is a good idea under certain conditions. The best time to carry an auxiliary parachute is during strong thermal days. It is doubtful whether reserve chutes of the type employed for hang gliding will open in less than 200 ft. of vertical descent. However, in lifting air this distance can be greatly reduced. Parachutes have definitely proven their worth to soaring pilots.

The line of attachment from the parachute should be securely hooked in the carabiner of your harness. This arrangement will keep the parachute with you even if your glider's suspension rope breaks. When you deploy your chute, you should throw it away from the glider if you can. The best designs employ a bag with a handle that lets you fling the package easily. The further you throw the parachute, the less chance there is of entanglement in the glider's cables and tubes.

Every pilot should practice parachute deployment. A good time to do this is every time the chute needs repacking. Hang a control bar up, climb in your harness and hook up in flying position. Imagine an emergency situation, then go for your chute, flinging it as far as possible. Have a friend time you and judge how far you can throw. A little practice will improve your performance considerably.

A parachute should be repacked every three months (ideally). Unfortunately, many pilots neglect to do this since a certified parachute repacker is often not readily available. For this reason, we recommend that each pilot learn to repack his own chute and make it a regular practice to do so. Request a certified repacker to show you how, or ask your local dealer or Regional Director to put on a parachute clinic.

A parachute must be treated with care if it is going to be reliable. Keep it out of excessive heat, sunlight and moisture. If it gets wet, air it out until it is completely dry to prevent fabric eating mildew from forming. It is a real letdown to toss a parachute that looks like a pair of moth eaten underwear.

The bridle leader of the parachute should run up the main strap of your harness. Tape or velcro the bridle to the harness strap to reduce drag and prevent an accidental deployment. Always run the bridle up the same side as the arm you throw with. This will keep the bridle from flipping you around with a violent jerk when the canopy opens. Practice throwing the chute with the same arm to the chosen side every time.

There are many chutes available today. Most are small (around 24 ft. diameter), light (6 to 7 pounds) and intended for low speed deployment. As long as you are with your glider and falling relatively slowly, there should be no strength problem. Larger and stronger parachutes are available for more cost and of course they weigh more.

Parachute design is as involved as hang glider design. A simple round canopy is an unstable drag devise–it wants to angle 45° to the path of descent. Cutting a circular hole in the top (apex) helps relieve this problem. Slower descent rates and improved stability are achieved by removing area from a few panels on one side of the chute. This allows the air to rush out which in turn creates thrust to move the parachute in the opposite direction. This forward motion creates lift just like it does for a hang glider.

Additional things to look for are mainly structural. The shroud lines should continue up through the canopy and should be present at every panel. V-tabs should be used where the shroud lines meet the canopy to distribute the loads evenly. Cloth tape should be sewn horizontally to keep the canopy from tearing in the event of a line-over (a line looped over the canopy during deployment can melt and rip the material through friction). All these features add weight, so you have to decide how much safety factor you want to add.

Landing with a chute deployed can be somewhat disconcerting. Invariably, the glider will be pitched downward at a very steep angle since the leader to the parachute is behind the sail. The best method of landing is to stand on the control bar during descent and jump off at the moment before touch-down. This is an unorthodox method of landing with a parachute, but remember, we are discussing an emergency situation. The parachute should be a silent partner in your flying. Don't acquire false confidence and fly in conditions you wouldn't enter without a chute.

MISCELLANEOUS EQUIPMENT

Another type of parachute used by cautious pilots or those getting used to a new glider's landing performance is a drag (or droque) chute. This is a small (about 3 ft. in diameter) canopy used to create a lot of additional drag which causes a steeper descent and shortens the runout on landing.

A drag chute is usually held in a small tube by the control bar. To deploy the chute, the pilot simply pulls on a chord and lets the chute unfold and slide back on a rear cable to the keel. The chute should only be deployed when on final approach as it hampers turning.

To control your glide path, simply alter your speed. At speeds near minimum sink, the chute has much less effect on performance. If you speed up, a much bigger dent in your glide ratio is made by the chute. To come down quickly, pull the bar in; to float along, slow up. Use the chute a few times in an open landing field to get a feel for its effect. Of course, you shouldn't rely on the chute to avoid the necessity of learning to set up perfect landings.

Another useful item is a pair of wheels. Pilots flying a glider for the first time or those that want to relieve some of the strain of carrying the heavier gliders find wheels to be a blessing. We highly recommend wheels on the control bar. The larger plastic wheels are good for rough terrain while the small (about 3" diameter) streamlined plastic wheels are lightest and create the least amount of drag.

An article of equipment that is necessary for any flight is a harness. Whether you fly supine or prone, your harness should be in top shape and of maximum comfort. If your harness doesn't fit properly, you will lose a lot of enjoyment on long duration flights. When buying a harness, hang in it for a period of time to see if it is designed properly for you (we're all built differently). There should be no excessive pressure points and you should be able to move freely.

If you are flying a supine harness, make sure you can sit up and lie back without pulling on the control bar or straining. A strap placed near the small of the back on the harness is the design factor that allows this. A feature to look for if you are buying a supine harness is curved bars on the main risers (see Figure 80). This allows you to pull the control bar closer to you– a necessity in strong conditions. To adjust a supine harness, simply raise or lower the suspension until the control bar is about even with your elbows when you are sitting up. With proper adjustment, a supine harness rides like an easy chair.

A prone harness requires a bit more attention. To be working properly, it should allow you to sit up and lie down with a minimum amount of effort, yet not require you to hold yourself in place in turbulence. This is mainly dependent on the adjustment and the amount of friction at the point where the shoulder to knee line passes through the top ring. If your main risers are too far back, you will tend to flop down; if they are too far forward, you will have to hold yourself down. The first thing in adjusting a harness is to make sure the main risers are in the right place. They should be at your body's center of gravity – usually just below the hip bones (balance yourself over a chair back to find your C.G). If you have a stirrup harness, lengthen or shorten the stirrup until the risers are placed right. If you have a knee – hanger harness, adjust the leg straps until the risers stay in place.

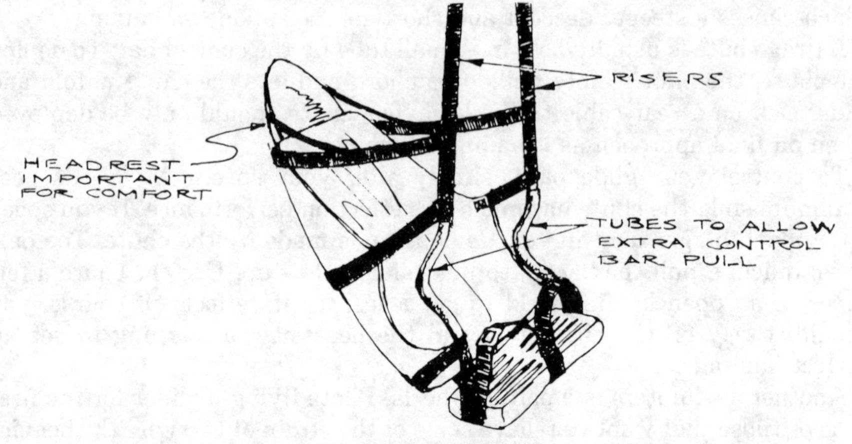

Figure 80 · Supine Harness

Swing your body back and check the clearance of your parachute. This should be 2 to 4 inches. Have someone hold the nose of your glider up until your parachute is over the control bar. The chute should clear by 2 to 4 inches. If not, adjust the main suspension loop at A and the shoulder strap at B as seen in Figure 81. Vary these adjustments until the clearance is proper and you are lying in a slightly feet high position. The latter is to minimize drag by aiming your body parallel to the airflow. If your harness has a stirrup, you may have to readjust it at this point (C). After flying for some time, recheck your adjustment to compensate for lines stretching.

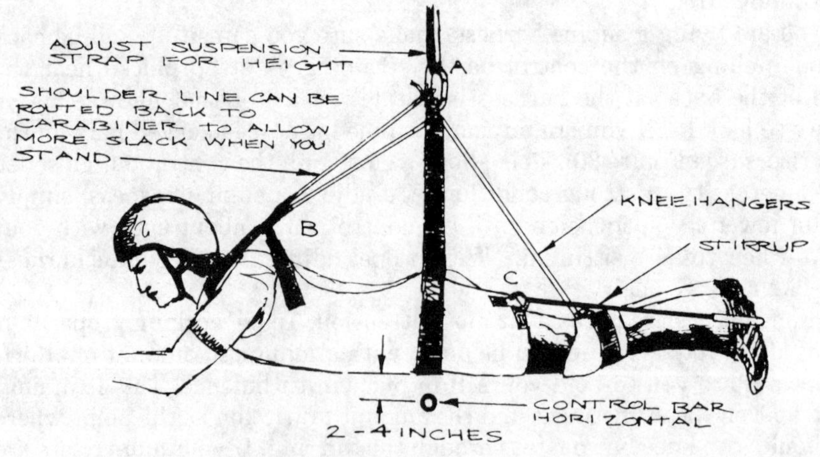

Figure 81 · Adjusting a Prone Harness

Stirrup harnesses occasionally present a problem in trying to step into them right after takeoff. One useful remedy is to put a plastic tube over the flexible stirrup lines so that the stirrup is stiff and remains in easy reach. Another popular idea is to hold the stirrup to one leg with a bungee or elastic band. The other foot then steps into the stirrup pulling it back into position. Try one of these methods – they make life a lot easier.

Most beginning pilots use a basic knee hanger or stirrup harness. As a pilot progresses, he may wish to purchase a "cocoon" harness. This design incorporates a bib that extends all the way to the toes, providing comfort and warmth on long high flights. Newer models also include an integrated parachute and ballast container on the front of the harness.

When purchasing a cocoon harness, be sure it is the right size. Since the length isn't adjustable, be sure to hang in the harness to see if the main suspension falls in the right place. Again, you shouldn't have a tendency to tip up or down. Try stepping in and out of the boot. You should be able to do this with ease.

Take offs and landings are more complicated with a cocoon harness; the boot can get in the way during the run. There are three methods of clearing the boot: drape it over the control bar, hold it in one hand, or hold it in the mouth. Each has their advantages – find the one that works for you. When landing, learn to alight with your feet spread apart and the boot dragging between your legs. The landing will require a waddling run unless you push out full. Practice these techniques at forgiving sites before attempting to launch or land at challenging areas in a newly acquired cocoon harness.

Your suspension line is one of the most important articles of equipment. Recommended is 9 mm purlon climbing rope. This rope is extremely strong and resists wear. You should not use a solid suspension – the elastic nature of the rope relieves loads in nasty air. Hook your rope where the manufacturer recommends. The lower you attach it, the more pendulum stability you have, but the harder your controls are. On the other hand, the lower your body is suspended (the longer your suspension lines are) the more stability and the lighter your controls will be. For this reason, tall control bars are desirable.

A cover often becomes a piece of flying equipment since many pilots strap it to their glider when flying sites with long turn around time. A lightweight, small rolling cover is desirable. If your glider didn't come with one, you can make one out of thin synthetic material. This "cross-country" cover can be used when flying, then covered over with your regular bag when traveling. A bit of convenience is always a great help.

Helmets are a part of your equipment that should be carefully selected, but require little attention subsequently. Of course, your helmet should be open at the ears to allow good hearing. If you are flying prone, you should look for a light helmet. A fatigued neck doesn't help your alertness. A solid shell helmet certainly provides more protection than a flexible type helmet.

THE GLIDER

The remaining part of your flying equipment (except for instruments which were covered in Chapter IV) is your glider. By the time you are reaching the advanced level in flying skill, you are probably flying a high performance model. The question is often asked "why can't a beginner or intermediate fly a high performance glider?" The answer is, they could if they had an instructor with them at all times for about a year of flying in progressively more challenging situations. This is rarely the case. A high performance glider is less forgiving. Tip stalls and slips have more severe results in advanced gliders. Take-offs are a bit more tricky and landings are an order of magnitude more difficult than with intermediate gliders. The problem with landings is setting up and maneuvering in tight spots. A high performance glider often wants to go up when you want to go down.

Assuming you can handle a high performance glider, you are shopping around for a new one, how should you go about finding the glider that's right for you? First of all, disregard all manufacturers' claims. You must fly or at least observe the glider you intend to buy to tell if it really suits your needs. Competition results do not necessarily indicate the best glider for all-around flying. Whether you are interested in competition, thermaling, ridge soaring or cross-country flying, you should look at as many gliders as you can to determine how they are going to work at your sites. Use the information in Chapter VI to evaluate the safety and flying possibilities of each glider. Rate each glider on the basis of handling, performance, safety and convenience, then select the one with the highest total score.

Once you have singled out the probable best choice, you must select the proper size. If you are very heavy or light, this may be a major consideration in which glider you select. Larger gliders will fly slower, sink slower, turn a smaller circle and take off easier. Smaller gliders will roll quicker, and penetrate better. A large glider is desirable for light thermals and ridge lift as well as for sink rate dominated competitions. In booming thermals, strong winds and for cross-country flying, a small glider is the choice.

Wing loading is the factor that determines how fast a glider flies. Some gliders are designed to fly with higher wing loadings. A glider with high performance but slow roll should be flown with a higher wing loading than an easy rolling glider. Pilots flying gliders with super roll rates tend to have lighter wing loadings; the only problem is, performance is poor at high speeds.

Since turning is such an important part of flying, you should consider the following when selecting a glider size. The slower your glider flys, the smaller your turn radius at a given bank angle. This is a simple law of physics. Flexible tips can help this matter by allowing you to slow even more in a turn. Figure 82(a) shows two gliders starting a turn at point A. The (larger) slower glider actually turns inside the faster glider. Another consideration is how quick the glider initiates a turn. In 82(b) we see two gliders starting a turn at point B, but one responding much quicker. The slow responding glider may miss a thermal entirely even if it can turn a smaller circle.

Obviously, you should talk to other pilots and watch a glider perform maneuvers before deciding how it responds. Use your common sense and the manufacturer's recommendations when selecting the right size glider for your flying. For safety reasons, your wing loading should be between 1 and 1.7 pounds per square foot. If you live in strong thermal country, you have no reason to fly a huge glider.

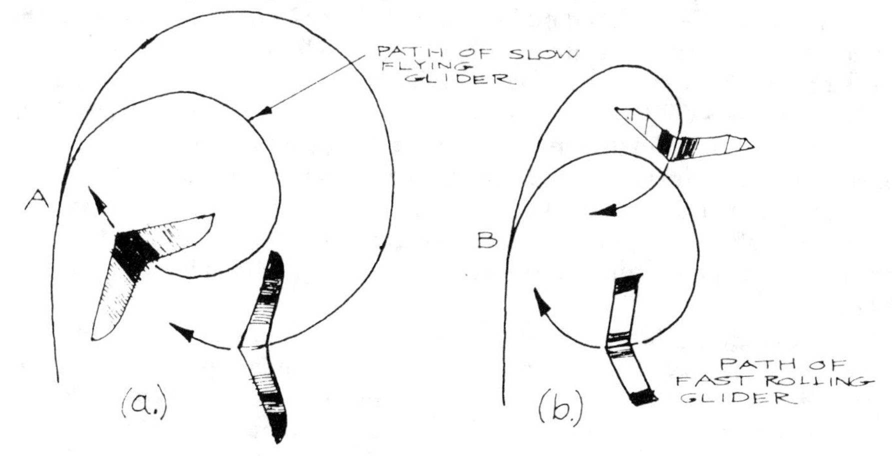

Figure 82 · Roll Response

TRIMMING YOUR GLIDER

Trimming a glider doesn't refer to cutting off some sail to increase the aspect ratio. To trim a glider you alter the balance and lift distribution so that it flies straight ahead at the right speed. Gliders get out of trim through stretching of the sail or deflexor cables, through weather changes or poor quality control during manufacture. A cold, wet day will tend to slacken the sail and make a glider fly nose light. A hot, dry day will do the opposite (dacron shrinks with heat). If your glider gets caught in a rain, expect it to be nose heavy (fast) when it dries.

To test a glider with deflexors for trim, you should fly it and sight down the deflexor cables. Let go of the control bar with at least 50 ft. ground clearance (to avoid ground effect) on a calm day. If your glider does not slow to a stall, check for an inherent turn first. If your glider does turn on its own, check for an imbalance in the rigging. To do this, have two helpers hold up the rear of the leading edges while you hold the nose. This puts tension on the deflexors and makes sighting more accurate. Even up both the down and side deflexors. Sight the sail and make sure it is exactly in the middle at the keel. With tight sails and raised keel pockets it is useless to sight for equal billow since it is hard to see and changes on both sides when you tighten one side deflexor. Now, with everything even, your glider should fly straight. If it doesn't, one wing is flying better (the lifting side). You can shift the sail towards the side the glider turns to by loosening the side deflexor on the rising side and tightening the side deflexor on the dropping side. However, this will make your sail slightly off-center. A better method than the above is to tighten the sail on the side the glider is turning to. As little as ¼ of an inch movement of the sail at the rear of the leading edge can make a noticeable difference.

One of the most important tools you can acquire is a simple spring scale. With this you can accurately set sail and deflexor tensions. You can also return to the same settings, in the future. To test the deflexors, remove the up and down deflexors then pull the side deflexors with the scale until the cable just leaves the post. Repeat the process on both sides until they read the same (with a raised keel pocket, tightening one will tighten the other). Now leave the side deflexors attached and equalize the down deflexors in the same manner. Finally, insert the negative deflexors and tighten them until they are snug. Once you have equalized everything, the glider should fly straight. If this is not the case, check for a bent tube, or assymetry. Assymetrical sails are more common than most pilots think. In this case, straighten the glider out by altering the side deflexors or adjusting sail tension.

Once the glider flies straight, correct the flying speed. Hands off, you should be flying between minimum sink and best glide. Speed the glider up by moving your center of gravity (hang point) forward. To slow the glider down, loosen the deflexors or move your hang point back. Moving back however, can lead to instability, so only a slight change is warranted.

Now that your glider is flying straight at the right speed, check it for straight ahead stalling. If it drops a wing when landing, that wing is stalling first. Simply tighten the deflexor on the opposite side to equalize the washout. This should not effect the turn much at all, but if it does, readjust the side deflexors.

The final thing to check for is equal setting of the defined tips. If one tip is set higher than the other, the glider will turn to that side at high speeds. Equalize their setting with spacers or by bending. Consult the manufacturer on proper tip angles. As you gain familiarity with your glider you can tell if it's in trim every time you fly. A simple small adjustment will then suffice to keep it flying perfectly. Remember, the out deflexors adjust for speed and turns while the down deflexors adjust for speed and stalls. Tightening the sail tension on one side will make the glider turn to the opposite side.

Newer gliders without deflexors must be trimmed by changing the sail position at the tip. Flight test your glider as outlined above, then tighten the sail at the end of the leading edge on the side that the glider turns towards in steady flight. If a wing drops consistantly on landing, this wing is stalling before the other. This can usually be remedied by loosening the sail on the dropping side. Some gliders with aluminum battens at the tip can be trimmed by changing the batten camber slightly. Be cautious of making too great a change, however, and only do so if you can't achieve hands off straight ahead flight by adjusting sail tension.

In the above type of glider, trim speed must be adjusted by changing C.G. or hang point. The ideal trim speed for thermaling is right at minimum sink. Since most newer designs suspend the pilot from the keel, some means of positive attachment must be used to keep the suspension loop in one place. Move the hang loop in ½ inch steps when making trim adjustments unless a large amount of change is obviously needed. Be sure to enlist the assistance of an experienced repairman if your trim problem is complex.

PERFORMANCE TUNING

Even though your glider is in perfect trim, chances are you can alter the tuning to achieve slightly better handling or performance. Manufacturers generally detune a glider to make it more docile. If this doesn't suit your needs, you can make some alterations.

To improve the glide ratio of your glider you can tighten the sail tension a bit at the end of the leading edges. This change reduces washout and improves the efficiency of the glider. You won't necessarily improve your sink rate, since you may remove camber, especially in sails with flexible battens. Note that this change may cause the glider to speed up, so be prepared to move your hang point rearward.

Another performance boosting trick available to those pilos with floating crossbar gliders is to adjust the crossbar fastener so that the crossbar opens more, thus tightening the sail. This again reduces washout and effectively creates more anhedral since the leading edges push out and down. Additional anhedral in a wing makes it roll easier, but may complicate turn coordination and require high-siding (moving to the high side of the control bar) when in the middle of a turn.

Changing the length of the side cables is a way to affect the dihedral of a glider directly. This practice requires a bit of equipment and precision workmanship, but is within the capabilities of many home experimenters. Length changes of as little as ¼ inch per side often produce noticeable differences. Some manufacturers will provide different length cables for different customer requirements. Generally, shorter cables make a glider less roll stable and easier to turn, up to a limit. Ask the manufacturer's advice before you experiment—he's probably already played around some. Be aware that changing the side cables usually changes the trim hang point. Shorter cables require moving the hang point back.

Another item to play with is battens. Batten tension can be tightened by adjusting the trailing edge ties. Tightening battens can tweak in a little performance sometimes. In general, battens should be checked with the factory supplied pattern and kept as close to original as possible. Battens in tight-sailed gliders often get flattened, so check your battens often for maximum performance. Some companies supply battens with different camber for slow speed operation. More camber in your battens will provide a better sink rate at the expense of top end performance. Caution: too much camber can seriously affect a glider's pitch stability, so consult the manufacturer before you try any alterations.

Some pilots have tried adding extra Mylar in the leading edge of their sail. This can provide a smoother airfoil, but also adds weight and stiffness. Try it if you like to experiment. Some pilots notice a difference.

All the above adjustments and alterations seem like great ways to improve our current gliders. However, without a doubt a manufacturer has fiddled and tweaked his design to get the best all around performance. It is doubtful that we can improve on this. However, since each performance factor is interrelated, we can usually get slight improvement in one place at the expense of another. In general, tightening the sail tension, crossbar tension, batten tension and adding Mylar will produce a stiffer glider that adversely affects handling. Every pilot has his own preferences, so there is room for experimentation. However, you must test fly carefully to see what you are improving and what you are deteriorating.

Remember, you can only get so much performance out of a given design; a sparrow is not an eagle. Enjoy the flying your glider has to offer once it is tuned to your desires.

CHAPTER VIII

COMPETITION

Competition means different things to different pilots. For some, it means a chance to exhibit their sport to the public in a safe but exciting manner. To others, competition is a means of comparing their equipment and skills with those of other pilots. Some pilots compete in hopes of doing well enough to land a job flying for a large manufacturer. Camaraderie and the chance to share flying experiences with old friends is what brings many to the meets. Whatever your reason for entering a hang gliding competition, you can't lose if you treat the event as an enjoyable learning experience.

The fact is, you can learn more about flying skills and hang gliding in general at a large meet than you can in six months of flying local hills. The exposure to new ideas, products and techniques that comes with the gathering of good pilots from around the country is well worth the work or expense of attending a meet. Even if you are simply a spectator or official, your hang gliding ability and experience will benefit by carefully observing the flying.

Competition can have its negative aspects. Certainly, the mental pressure can be great if you are pushing yourself to do well. Usually you are required to take-off in a prescribed time period. For most events you have to forget about that thermal you just passed through and stick to a prescribed course. You cannot relax and enjoy the scenery in the heat of competition. Official judgment and scorekeeping is sometimes not up to your expectations. Often conditions are unflyable, yet you must wait at the launch in hopes of improvement when normally you would be off relaxing with friends. Flying in front of crowds may bring out your worse performance, or cause you to overperform. The pace of competition is usually not leisurely.

Despite all these drawbacks, you can compete with enjoyment if you have the right attitude. If you are serious about winning a competition, you should ask yourself why. If the answer is along the lines of personal improvement, then you probably are on the right track. Now carefully examine your experience and skills. If you have not been flying for years and are not totally at home in the air, then you should not expect to finish near the top. Relax and enjoy the flying, the people and the parties that are ever-present. Only after you have a lot of competition experience should you start challenging yourself to do better. At this point you will have the skills and mental control necessary to handle the challenge. Like any trained athlete, you will have to discipline yourself and avoid the late night cavorting. However, placing at the top in a series of meets will be well worth the effort of self control.

PREPARING FOR COMPETITION

To start developing your competition skills, participate in local meets. These are generally low-key, inexpensive affairs that can provide you with a lot of experience useful later. If local meets aren't being sponsored, plan one yourself, then cajole a non-flying friend to run it. Keep the costs and obligations at a minimum and you'll be able to hold several meets a season without overburdening yourself. Fly-ins with one or two tasks that pilots can try at their leisure are minimum hassle, maximum enjoyment events. If your main interest is to gain competition experience, don't worry about attracting spectators and making money – leave that to promoters. If your sites are not suitable for competition, you can at least have friendly rivalry with your regular flying buddies to see who can land closest to a spot, or stay up the longest in non-soaring conditions. At the very least, you should practice honing your skills on every flight you take.

What skills should you practice? Most obviously, take-off and landing skills. In fact, these portions of a flight are so important that they will be treated later in separate sections. Turns of all types are also top priority. First, practice simple turns of varying degree bank. Coordinate each turn carefully to produce minimum altitude loss. Do this in all types of conditions – light winds, strong winds, calm and rough air. Next, practice slipping turns to allow you to control your altitude on landing approaches. Do this with plenty of ground clearance and don't allow too much speed build-up.

Of great importance is 360 ° turns. Both as a pylon maneuver and for thermaling. Practice slow, wide 360s and fast tight ones. Try starting with a slow, shallow bank turn and gradually steepen the bank until you are in a tight 360. Also try the opposite: start a fast steep turn, then gradually reduce your bank and slow up to a flat 360.

Another important thing to practice is reversing turns. Once you are turning one way, see how fast you can reverse directions. You should repeat all of these turn variations over and over until you feel completely at home in the air. You should be able to turn whenever you want to at as steep a bank as possible. Each turn should be coordinated with a minimum of altitude loss.

You must try the above maneuvers in varying wind conditions. You should be able to do a series of 360s or alternating 180s without drifting downwind. This requires varying your turn a bit (see Handling Tasks). You should feel at ease initiating either upwind, downwind or crosswind turns. Most pilots have a preferred side to turn toward. This is a force of habit and due to a greater strength in one arm. Practice turning toward your "bad" side until you have no preference. Good turning ability is a matter of skill and judgment. Practice turns assiduously until you can place your glider exactly where you want it in the three-dimensional airspace.

The next thing to practice is speed control. This means learning the cardinal speeds on your glider. Not only must you know how to fly at minimum sink and maximum glide, but you should learn how to vary these speeds as required for different wind and lift conditions. The material in Chapters I and III should be reviewed and applied to your practice.

Working lift patterns and thermals is, of course, an integral part of a competition pilot's skills. Spend as much time as you can riding the lift. Think about the air in relation to the terrain while you are flying. Look for relationships between the location of thermals and potential sources as well as the amount of lift available as the size or steepness of the ridge changes. Eventually you will be able to read an area and find the best location of lift a majority of the time.

If you are serious about competition, you should get yourself and your equipment in the best physical condition possible. Hang gliding does not require a tremendous amount of exertion, but it is a fact that the more physically fit you are, the better you will cope with the stresses and demands of daily competition. Not only your alertness, but your reflexes and judgment will benefit from a premeet exercise program. For our purposes here, running can't be beat. Many top hang gliding competitors subscribe to a regular jogging program.

To get your glider in shape, you obviously want to trim it perfectly. You should also tune it for the maximum peformance according to the type of meet you are entering. If a lot of maneuvers are required, handling is the most important asset of your glider. Contact the manufacturer of your particular ship and request information on the best tuning possible. Be sure to do this ahead of time so you have time to familiarize yourself with any flying differences.

One of the most important pre-contest preparations is developing an overall competition plan. This means visiting the site ahead of time to get some practice in, learn the unique features of the terrain and develop a method of attack. You can start this process at home by practicing flying to a specific flight plan or course. See how well you can stick to your original intentions. This practice will simulate a prescribed task, which is always a part of competition.

Your overall philosophy should be to fly conservative and consistent in the initial rounds. Generally, the pilot that flies well and makes sure he earns points every flight will end up near the top. Too often pilots try for an extra turn or pylon and end up with a bad flight score. Once you are in the finals, or if you absolutely must maximize a task to stay in the running, then you should "go for it." This doesn't mean fly recklessly, but you should try that extra turn if there's any chance of making it. The greater the number of pilots and the greater the number of flights in the meet, the better this competition plan works. And of course, the more preparing you do, the better you will perform.

TAKING OFF

Every flight is affected by the quality of the take-off that begins it. This is especially true at low sites. You cannot afford to have poor take-off technique if you are competing. On a slope launch, the faster you can get the glider moving by running, the better. You can use speed to gain extra altitude if necessary. There is nothing to be gained by performing a slow launch, even in lift.

To run properly, you should have a method of holding the control bar that gives you perfect pitch control. The technique shown in Figure 83 is by far the best for both prone and seated. Both arms are around the down tubes and you can easily run vigorously. You can hold the proper angle of attack even if a gust hits you. Once you are in the air, drop your hands to the horizontal bar one at a time for proper control.

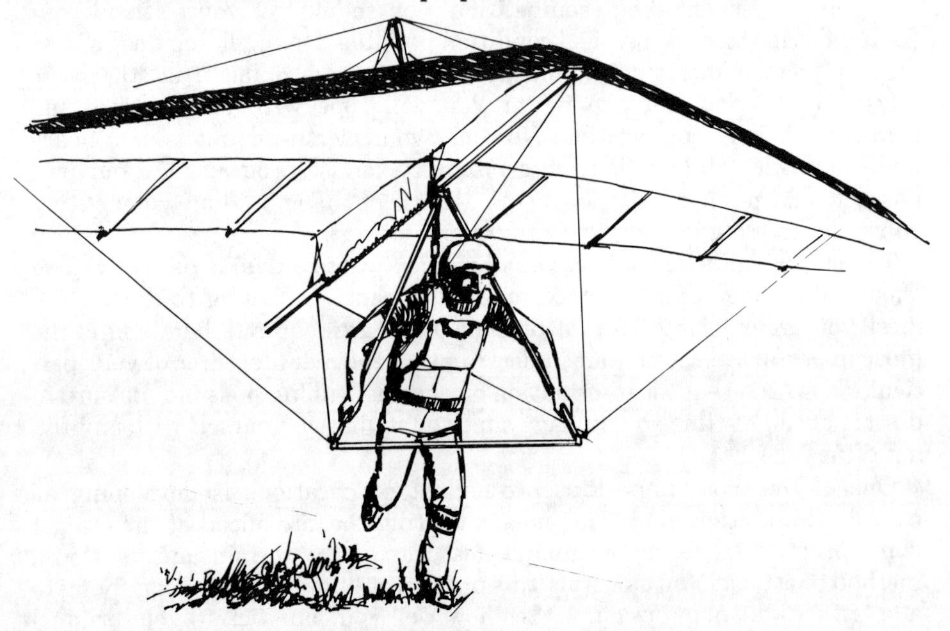

Figure 83 · Holding the Control Bar

On a cliff launch, use the above method with wire men in strong conditions or run hard in light winds (below 8 mph). Keep your nose down when performing a running cliff launch. If your nose is a bit too low you will regain most of your original altitude when you pull out of the ensuing dive. If your nose is too high, you will stall and lose a lot of altitude. Stalled cliff launches are also dangerous.

In light winds on both cliff and slope launches, angle your run towards your flight path. You'll be surprised to find how much time or altitude this simple technique will save you. If you fly with a stirrup harness, don't make the mistake of stepping into the stirrup before you are stabilized in flight. Too many pilots stall or delay turning while trying to instantly "prone out."

Of course, with practice you can locate and use your stirrup in a smooth automatic motion.

Special attention should be paid to wire launches. These are launches that require an assistant to hold the nose wires (and possibly side wires) of the glider until the pilot gets situated properly in the airstream. The factor that determines whether or not a wire assist is warranted is the wind velocity. On a smooth slope wind, a pilot may be able to launch himself into a breeze of 15 mph or more, but on a sharp cliff even an 8 mph wind can cause ground handling problems.

The secret of a safe, successful cliff launch in higher winds is getting as much of the glider as possible into the airstream. This can only be done if a nose-wire man with a secure rope is employed. No sane assistant will want to back up to a sheer cliff with a bucking glider in his grasp unless he is tied fast to a tree with stout rope. Secure him first, then he will secure you with his careful control of your nose angle.

Side wire men should be used if the wings are rocked in the cliff-side rotor. Once you are in position in the airstream at the edge of the cliff, have the nose man lift or lower the glider until he feels neither up nor down pressure. This indicates the glider is not being lifted or forced down by the wind. If one wing lifts, the nose man should rotate the nose so that the opposite wing comes forward, thus equalizing the airflow over both wings. When the pilot has the glider totally under his control he should tell the side men to release (they should remain ready to grab the glider if a gust arises). Without too much hesitation the pilot should then tell the nose man to release with a loud clear command, such as READY, GO. As soon as the nose man lets go he should dive out of the way and the pilot should launch. Any hesitation increases the chance of an errant gust upsetting his launch. In competition, of course, a bad launch is particularly undesirable since a broken glider means a loss of a flight or the entire meet.

Try to get to the launch site early and set up well ahead of your time to fly. This allows you a spell to relax, review the task, refine your flight plan and watch other pilots in the course. Watching the progress of other pilots is most important. From their flights you can learn of the presence of lift, sink or turbulence as well as see what you should expect your glider to do. A quick, convenient glider is a real asset in competition. The sooner you finish your set-up and preflight, the more time you have to pay attention to the challenge of the flight.

LANDING

The first thing you should do when you arrive at a competition site is walk the landing area. You should look for hazards and the best possible approaches. Imagine the wind blowing from different directions and set up a landing pattern for each condition. Look for sloping ground and take this into consideration when you determine how high to be on your final approach. As the competition progresses, modify your original diagnosis to take into account any unseen difficulties (unexpected sink or lift). Watch your fellow competitors. If they are consistently overshooting or undershooting the landing zone, set up lower or higher respectively.

The type of landing approach you use depends on your glider and the task requirements. If, for instance, you are merely in a glide ratio contest, you want to keep the glider flying as far as possible. You then fly your best glide speed until you are near the ground, pushing out gradually as you get lower. When you are just about to stall, throw the bar forward hard and pull your legs up under you. If you do this properly you will perform a stand up landing and fly as far over the ground as possible.

If the competition task is a spot landing or a small scoring zone, the technique is entirely different. First, you must set up your approach. There are two recommended methods for doing this. The first is shown in Figure 84(a). Here the pilot makes a series of turns downwind of the target to lose altitude then makes his final approach once he judges he has the right height. He must be sure the turns at A and B are greater than 180° or he will gradually creep up to the target and limit his options. The best way to perfect this technique is to imagine soaring a ridge stretching between points A and B. Once on final, you can vary your glide slope by various means (see below) to hit the bulls eye. Use this spot landing method in wide open fields with a quick handling glider.

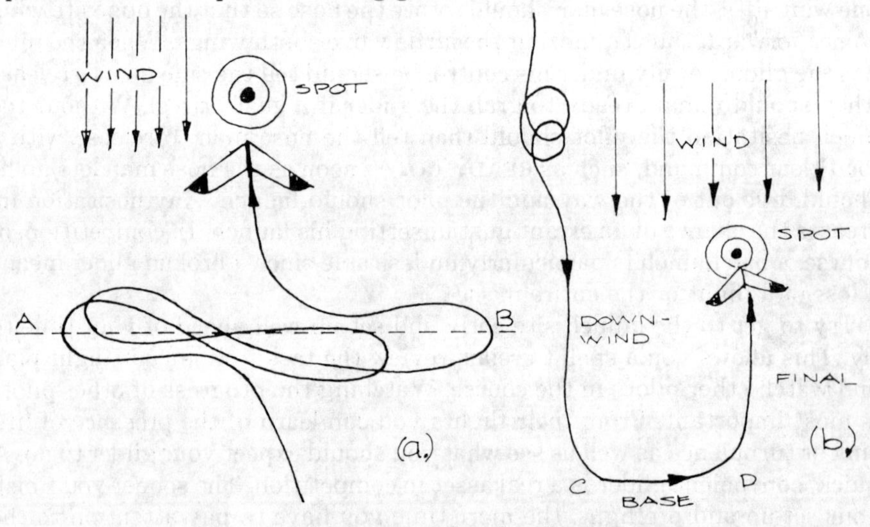

Figure 84 · Spot Landing

If the field is narrow or your glider is not very responsive, you should use the traditional aircraft landing approach. This is shown in 84(b). Here the pilot makes a downwind, base and final approach, all the time keeping his eye on the spot and judging his distance from the target. He has many options. He can lenghthen or shorten his downwind and base legs, and make his turns at C and D efficient or slipping. If space allows, a combination of the two methods can be used, with the first method being inserted in the final leg of the second method.

When shooting for a spot, *do not* do a 360° turn on one side of the target.

This breaks your eye contact with the target and can disorientate you. Keeping a close watch on the target will assure you the most consistent spot landing. Also, beware of wind gradients in the landing area. Strong horizontal winds or no wind at all can have the same effect of dropping you short of the target. The first condition impedes your forward progress, while the second situation destroys your altitude as you pull in to avoid stalling in the gradient. Check the windsocks around the landing area often, before and during your flight to keep a good handle on the wind. Of course, if they are varying frequently you have to trust your luck and your quick turning reflexes.

Once the pilot is on his final approach, he should vary his glide according to how high he ends up. To vary glide path, he can vary his drag, his angle of attack, or both. To vary drag, a drag chute can be deployed, or the stand-up posture can be assumed (see Figure 85). Of course, diving faster than best glide speed will steepen the glide path. This procedure is best used in combination with increasing the drag, so that when the nose is raised the glider doesn't have a lot of excess energy to float across the target.

Figure 85 - The Stand-up Drag Position

You cannot get too much practice using the stand-up drag technique. You should become completely relaxed doing turns in this position so that you can perform your complete landing approach standing up. This is useful in tight landing fields.

The lower your harness allows you to hang, the easier it is to control in the stand-up position. Also, the hands should not be too high or roll forces will be very hard. On the other hand, when flaring for a landing, most high performance gliders require a full hard push out that can only be accomplished with the hands held high up on the control bar. Consequently the hands should be moved up just before flaring for landing.

If you have trouble preventing a nose-in, try keeping one foot in your stirrup to keep from dropping down when you stand up so that you can reach high and flare. With practice, you can drop down when setting up the landing with the leg still in the stirrup bent, then push up when you get ready to flare. Flare with a full hard push forward and up when you run out of airspeed and kick out of the stirrup just as you alight.

HANDLING TASKS

There are as many different forms of competition as there are sites and flying conditions. Older type of contests and some fly-ins make use of the following tasks: pylon turns, distance runs, duration events, speed runs and cross country events.

Pylon turns can either be a slow flight event, or a fast slalom run. In slow pylon turns, the task usually consists of a figure 8 or a cloverleaf pattern. The object is to round as many pylons as possible. Besides the necessity of making numerous tight reversing turns, the biggest problem is accounting for wind drift. In Figure 86 we see a pilot rounding a figure 8 course. With the wind in the given direction the pilot must make un upwind turn at A and B and a downwind turn at C and D. To keep his ground track above the pylons, he must elongate his turns at A and B and only turn a small amount at C and D. If the wind was from the direction parallel to the line intersecting the two pylons, he would have to carry his upwind run well past the upwind pylon to keep from shooting past the gate between the pylons when he turns downwind.

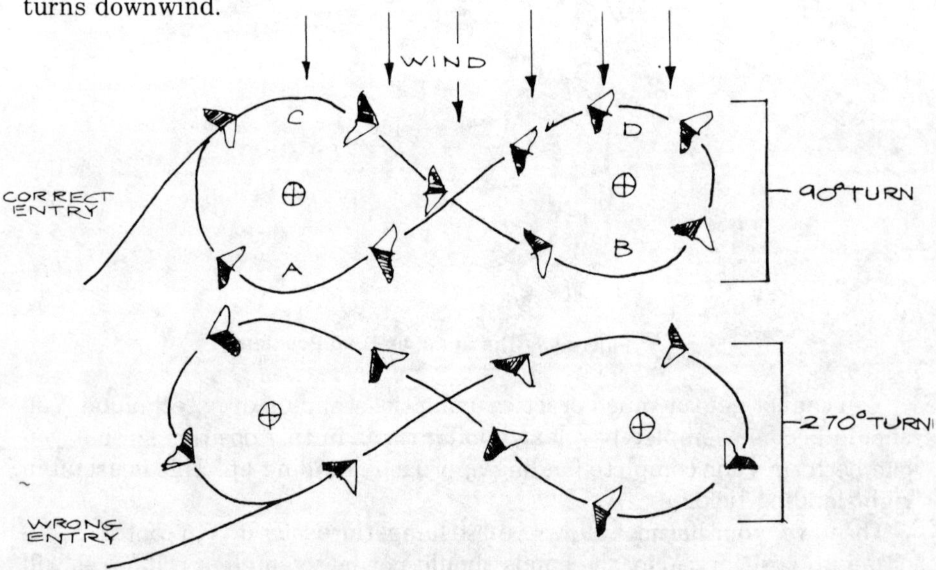

Figure 86 · Figure 8 Pylons

In the figure, we see there is a right way and a wrong way to enter the pylon course. The correct way is to enter the course on the upwind side of the pylons. The reason for this is that much less turning is required between point A and B with the upwind entry, since the glider must crab into the wind. With the correct entry, the pilot only has to turn about 90 ° to get around the pylon, while the downwind entry requires about a 270 ° turn for the same flight path.

How tight should your turns be around the pylons? That depends on the conditions. As mentioned, in a wind you have to vary your angle of bank to account for drift. In a calm, the most efficient turn is a 45° bank. This loses the least amount of altitude for a given turn. However, if reversing turns are required, a 45° bank will take too long to straighten out. Use a lesser bank in pylon turns unless multiple 360° turns are required.

If you are high above the pylons, fly slowly and make wide circles. It is hard to determine exactly where you are at altitude and you do not want to risk missing a pylon. For obvious reasons, a prone pilot has a much easier job of spotting pylons than does a seated pilot. Consider this when starting to fly competition.

Slalom type pylon courses are fun and fairly easy. There is, however, a little technique involved. You should enter the pylons wide and cut the gate tight when exiting. This gives you the best acceleration and the shortest actual flying distance (see Figure 87). Use this technique when rounding pylons in a folded distance course. Often a small bit of extra efficiency means the difference in winning or placing down the line.

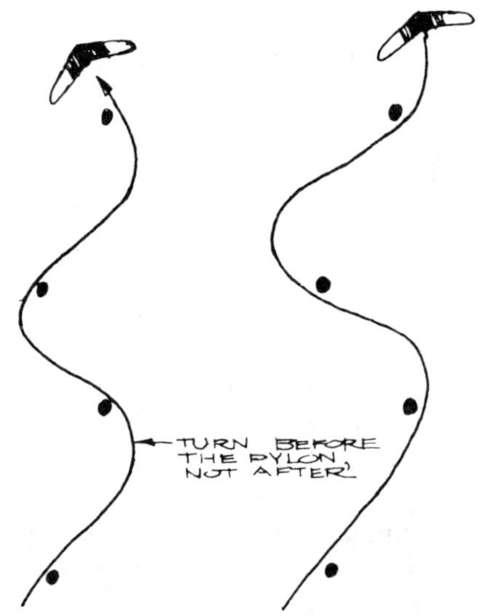

Figure 87 · Running Pylons

Distance runs are fun to fly. The technique for best performance is simply fly the speed for best glide path over the ground according to your glider's polar (see Chapter III). In general, this means slow up in the lift near the take-off, speed up in the upwind runs and slow up in the downwind portions of the course. Practice this at your home site and you should do quite well, even if you can't find the exact best speed to fly.

Timed runs consist of duration events and speed runs or a combination of these. In duration events, you must simply fly your minimum sink speed unless you are in localized sink. In this case, speed up to get out of the sinking air, then slow again in lift or neutral air. Watch your vario, look for weather signs and observe the flights of other pilots to see if the conditions warrant flying at any speed other than your minimum sink speed.

Speed runs can be unnerving (and unsafe) in turbulent air. Hopefully competition Safety Directors will acknowledge this fact and limit speed flying to smooth conditions. To fly fast you have only two options. Pull in the bar or add weight. A ballast container is a handy item for changing your wing loading. You can keep it empty for the slow flight events then fill it for the penetration events. Whenever you are flying a speed run or a distance course, minimize your body's drag by pulling your elbows in, pointing your toes and avoiding extraneous movement.

CROSS COUNTRY TASKS

Modern competitions utilize open distance tasks (pilot flying the furthest wins), time to a goal (minimum time wins) or closed course cross country task (fastest time through the course wins). In all the above, the main criteria is ridge soaring and thermaling skills. You must have a bit of luck and a lot of experience soaring in different conditions.

There are two types of launch situations in common use. The first is an "open window." With this type of launch, pilots can take off whenever they choose. Thus, the burden is on the pilot to use all his knowledge of local conditions and thermal generation to pick the best launch time. Local pilots (not flying in competition) can often provide good weather information. Thermals are generally best in the hottest part of the day. This is not noon, but in the early afternoon (from 1 to 3 o'clock) due to a slight lag process. Often, you can time the thermal cycles, or see the effect of a thermal approaching as it rustles ground cover. If the thermals aren't too strong, you can launch into a large one and get your initial lift for your journey.

Once you are on your way you must make maximum use of your cross country skills. If time is a factor, speeds to fly and the utilization of only the best lift should be considered. The cross country sections in Chapter V will point out the best flying techniques.

The second launch format is one-on-one. In this case, two pilots launch simultaneously and the winner advances in the standings to fly another winning competitor. The initial philosophy here is to climb higher than your opponent as quickly as possible. As soon as you accomplish this, continue trying to climb but do not get too far from your opponent or he may hit a stray thermal that carries him well above you and puts you out of the running.

As soon as you gain enough height to make the course or first timed pylon with little doubt, do so. If your opponent is higher than you, wait until he is turned the other way before you start your run. This is a good play even if he is lower.

Again, if you are higher than your opponent, stick like glue. If he passes up lift, stay and work it only if it's highly likely that there's no other good patch around. Many a contest has been lost because a lower pilot flew away to a lucky bubble. On the other hand, if you are lower, you are free to explore the air according to your own skills and judgment. Since you don't have to pay as much attention to your opponent, you can work small patches and gamble a little in your search for lift. Keep an eye out for your opponent's wiley ways and follow him through the course if there is a reasonable chance of finding lift along the way. In this situation it's obvious that you can get a lot of help by watching the other pilots flying before you.

In some competitions, the pilot that stays up the longest wins if lift is not adequate to complete the course. In this case, it often helps to fly away from your opponent to find the best air you can. If he insists on following you, fly a zig-zag path. This will require him to constantly pass through your wake turbulence if he intends to remain your shadow. A zig-zag path will also give you a greater chance of locating a small thermal.

If you and your opponent are on the course heading for a pylon and you encounter lift, it is rarely wise to stop and climb higher unless it is obvious that neither of you will make the pylon. The reason for this is that the distance lost while circling in lift cannot be made up without losing a lot of altitude due to the high sink rate related to high speed. Even in the best performing hang gliders, a thermal would have to be well over 600 fpm before it would provide any advantage.

It should be obvious that one-on-one and competition flying in general requires a lot of thoughtful observation and tactical calculation. You must be prepared to alter your original intentions with quick in-flight decisions at all times. Lift and sink are often unpredictable, but the experienced competitor knows the best possible way to handle either condition.

Certainly, a large element of chance determines the winner of any hang gliding competition. However, good pilots will finish near the top due to their consistency, tenacity and elimination of flying errors. If you get "conditioned out" or make an unwise decision, learn from your mistakes, but smile and accept your fate. Remember, we are all flying for enjoyment. Next time, be determined to correct your errors and pray for better winds.